TIGLATH PILESER III

COLUMBIA
UNIVERSITY PRESS
SALES AGENTS

NEW YORK:
LEMCKE & BUECHNER
30–32 West 27th Street

LONDON:
HENRY FROWDE
Amen Corner, E.C.

TORONTO:
HENRY FROWDE
25 Richmond St., W.

*CONTRIBUTIONS TO ORIENTAL HISTORY
AND PHILOLOGY*

No. V.

TIGLATH PILESER III

BY

ABRAHAM S. ANSPACHER, Ph.D.

New York

COLUMBIA UNIVERSITY PRESS

1912

Set up and electrotyped.   Published November, 1912.

Norwood Press
J. S. Cushing Co. — Berwick & Smith Co.
Norwood, Mass., U.S.A.

NOTE

The following thesis by Dr. A. S. Anspacher gives the most succinct account of the reign of Tiglath Pileser III which has yet been attempted. The author has systematically endeavored to place a number of localities, mentioned in the documents of this great Assyrian king, and in so doing he has made a distinct contribution to ancient geography. Tiglath Pileser's map has always been somewhat uncertain, and, in his work, Dr. Anspacher has succeeded not only in establishing several new locations, but he has traced, more carefully than has been done hitherto, the routes of march of the principal campaigns inaugurated by this notable conqueror.

In compiling the tale of an ancient nation, it is necessary to specialize on the material of each period, and also on that of each important reign ; and this is what Dr. Anspacher has done. While it is true that all the riddles of the history of a vanished people can never be satisfactorily solved, a careful study, such as this dissertation undoubtedly is, cannot fail to be of value to the historian.

J. DYNELEY PRINCE.

COLUMBIA UNIVERSITY,
NEW YORK CITY.

INTRODUCTION

The attempt to solve all the problems connected with the life and history of Tiglath Pileser III can never be fully successful as long as we remain without new inscriptional material by means of which to fill in the lacunæ which so unfortunately abound in the existing tablets. With but one exception, all the inscriptions which we now possess were found by Layard in the Southwest Palace of Nimrod. Some of the tablets came originally from the Northwest, some from the Central Palace; and since all three of the mounds which mark the sites of these three palaces have been thoroughly explored, it is perhaps too much to hope that more records of Tiglath Pileser's reign will come down to us.

This thesis is an attempt to fix in some detail the principal facts in the history of Tiglath Pileser III. Although every standard work on Assyrian history has some pages devoted to this theme, no author has treated it with such detail as to present the full story. The entire subject has appealed to me as one deserving far more consideration than is usually accorded to it in the histories. The reign of Tiglath Pileser III was from one point of view the most important in Assyrian history, and the revolutionary tendencies which characterized it are of as much importance to civilization as they were to the then welfare of Assyria itself. It needed a revolution to make the conservative Assyrian politicians of the time realize that the very existence of the state was in danger. To curtail the immense revenues of the priests so that sufficient means to carry on the extensive military operations always necessary to Assyria's safety might never be lacking was the immediate aim of the revolution. That result it speedily achieved. But from the viewpoint of world history it also accomplished a far more valuable work, in that it gave Tiglath Pileser the opportunity so to shape Assyria's policies as to give her a longer lease of life than would otherwise have been hers.

When Tiglath Pileser III came to the throne, Assyria was already beginning to succumb to the forces of decay. Her dependencies were being gradually taken from her, and her armies were meeting frequent reverses. It needed a great warrior and statesman to save her, not only for herself, but for the accomplishment of her cultural work. The value of this king to civilization, therefore, lies not in the fact of his extensive conquests themselves, but rather in the fact that without him Assyria would not have endured long enough to bequeath anything to the world.

The proper fixing of the geographical locations mentioned in the inscriptions is of prime importance. I have, wherever possible, tried to determine these and also the routes of march by the aid of all the historical inscriptions that were available to me, and believe that I have fixed some of these with exactness. One fact I wish to note here. At first thought it would seem that the Arabic geographers should yield material for the determination of some of the localities in question, but on the contrary no such aid is forthcoming. They deal with a later

period of the history of Western Asia, and only a very
few of the geographical names of the times of which they
treat preserve even a reminiscence of old Assyrian nomen-
clature.

In conclusion I wish to thank Professor Prince, under
whom I have studied my major subject, Assyriology, and
whose aid and suggestion as well as able instruction have
given to my work whatever value it may possess.

To Professor Richard Gottheil I also owe a debt of
gratitude for many helpful suggestions, and have much
pleasure in expressing my appreciation and gratitude.

ABRAHAM S. ANSPACHER.

CONTENTS

PRINCIPAL ABBREVIATIONS

Assy. Can. . . . . G. Smith, Assyrian Eponym Canon, 1869.

Disc. . . . . G. Smith, Assyrian Discoveries, 1875.

Br. . . . . Rudolph E. Brünnow, Classified List, 1889.

Rost . . . . Paul Rost, Die Keilschrifttexte Tiglat-Pileser's III. Band I: Einleitung, Transcription und Uebersetzung, Wörterverzeichniss mit Commentar. Band II: Autographierte Texte, 1893.

Ann. . . . . Annals: in Rost, Band I. pp. 2 ff.

Th. A. . . . . . . Die Thontafelinschrift, obverse; in Rost, Band I. pp. 55–69.

Th. R. . . . . . Die Thontafelinschrift, reverse; in Rost, Band I. pp. 70–77.

Pl. I. . . . . . . Platteninschrift von Nimrud, No. I; in Rost, Band I. pp. 42–47.

Pl. II. . . . . . Platteninschrift von Nimrud, No. II; in Rost, Band I. pp. 48–53.

Kl. I. . . . . . . Kleinere Inschriften; in Rost, Band I. pp. 78–83.

Kl. II. . . . . . Kleinere Inschriften; in Rost, Band I. pp. 84–85.

KAT.[2] . . . . . Schrader, Keilinschriften und das Alte Testament, 2d ed., 1883.

KB. . . . . Schrader, Keilinschriftliche Bibliothek, Vols. I–IV.

KGF. . . . . . Schrader, Keilinschriften und Geschichtsforschung, 1878.

Kritik. . . . . . Schrader, Zur Kritik der Inschriften Tiglath-Pileser's II, des Asarhaddon und des Ashurbanipal, 1879.

Forsch. . . . . Winckler, Altorientalische Forschungen.

Untersuchgn. . Winckler, Untersuchungen zur altorientalische Geschichte, 1889.

Lay. . . . . Layard Inscriptions in the Cuneiform Character, 1851.

Paradies. . . . Delitzsch, Wo lag das Paradies ? 1881.
Sulm. . . . . . Billerbeck, Das Sandschak Suleimania, 1898.
R. . . . . Rawlinson, Cuneiform Inscriptions of Western Asia.
RP. . . . . . . Records of the Past.
PSBA. . . . . . Proceedings of the Society of Biblical Archæology.
ZA. . . . . . . Zeitschrift für Assyriologie.
JRAS. . . . . . Journal of the Royal Asiatic Society.

TIGLATH PILESER III

CHAPTER I

THE SOURCES

From the time of the destruction of the Babylonian Empire until the middle of the last century, when Layard began his excavations, Tiglath Pileser III[1] was known only because of the mention of his name in a few Biblical verses.[2] Nothing was certain about him, except that a king of that name had ruled in Assyria and had made his power felt in Palestine. All knowledge of his history had passed from human memory, and even the inscriptions which finally proved to be his, when they were unearthed and deciphered, presented many a puzzling problem. The mutilated condition in which the tablets were found did not, at the time, promise much for a future solution of the difficulties; besides which, one of the tablets — the longest inscription — was so badly cracked and broken in shipment to the British Museum that many attempts to correct the first faulty piecing together were for a long time unsuccessful. When this

[1] Schrader, *KAT.*[2] p. 240 and note, reads the name "Tu-kul-ti (Tuk-lat)-habal-i-šarra"; he translates, "Trust (*i.e.* Object of Trust) is the Son of the Šarra Temple." Note *ABK.* p. 148, No. 9, and p. 151: the "Son of the Šarra Temple is the God Adar"; the basic meaning of the name, therefore, is "Trust is Adar."

[2] 2 K. xv. 29 and xv. 7; 1 Chr. v. 6, 26; 2 Chr. xxviii. 20. The form *Tiglath Pilneser* in Chronicles is due to "an accidental corruption of the familiar name at the hands of the Chronicler or of his Midrashic source." (Kittel, *Chron. Heb. SBOT.* 68.) He was known as Tiglath

1

had finally been accomplished, it was discovered that about a hundred lines were missing altogether.

When Layard had in the course of his excavations reached what he afterwards called "the Southwest Palace of Nimrod," he found that the whole interior of one of the large halls remained "fairly intact,"[3] and that it was panelled with slabs brought from elsewhere. Some of the slabs came originally from the Northwest, some from the Central Palace. "The bas-reliefs always, when left entire, turned toward the wall of sun-dried brick, . . . and upon the faces of most of the slabs forming wall E were the marks of a chisel; . . . the bas-reliefs had been purposely destroyed. Only parts of the wall F had been finished. Many of the slabs not having been used and still lying in the centre of the chamber, . . . it was evident that these were entire, having only suffered from fire. They were, moreover, arranged in rows with great regularity, and, in one or two instances, heaped the one above the other."

The analysis of these inscriptions, at whose interpretation several partial attempts were made before Schrader's authoritative work, was all rendered secondary by that scholar's investigation.[4] Schrader divided the inscriptions into Annals and the so-called *Prunkinschriften:* the

Pileser II, until, in 1886, Th. G. Pinches, in "Guide to the Kouyunjik Gallery," p. 9, No. 72, described an inscription of Ramman-Nirâri II, which showed that a grandfather of that king was also called Tiglath Pileser. This is the second king of the name, and our king is, therefore, the third. Winckler published the inscription in *KB.*[1] pp. 48–49, and in *ZA.* II. p. 311.

[3] "Nineveh and its Remains," vol. II. pp. 27 ff.

[4] *Zur Kritik der Inschriften Tiglath Pileser's II, des Asarhaddon und des Asurbanipal,* in *Kön. Akademie der Wissenschaft zu Berlin,* 1879. A description of all the inscriptions published up to 1886 is given in

last being arranged not chronologically, but geographically. Both have been published, transliterated, and translated in part, by many scholars. Schrader divides the Annals into those composed of 7, 12, and 16 lines, respectively. Of the seven-line inscriptions (seven in number), Layard published five.[5] They are those which in his collection are designated as 69, A, 1; 69, A, 2; 69, B, 1; 69, B, 2; and 34, B. The last was translated by Smith,[6] and the remaining two inscriptions of this set were published by the same author.[7] The second group is made up of twelve-line inscriptions, although one, Lay. 45, B, in its present condition contains only eight lines, the first four being broken away. Another, III R 9, No. 1,[8] is so badly mutilated that not a single line remains intact. Lay. 50, A (III R 9, No. 3, p. 41–52) is in a very fair condition and is continued in Lay. 50, B, and Lay. 67, A; both these last being written on one stone; while Lay. 67, B, is a continuation of Lay. 67, A; making of the four inscriptions a complete sub-group. Lay. 51, A, and 51, B,[9] are written on tablets the last half of which is entirely broken away, but what remains is perfectly legible; Lay. 51, B, being damaged to the extent of only a small lacuna in the last line. Lay. 52, A, and Lay. 52, B,[10] are fairly well preserved and form a continuous narrative.[11] The

Bezold, *Kurzgefasster Überblick über die Babylonisch-Assyrische Literatur.* (Leipzig, 1886.)

[5] " Inscriptions in the Cuneiform Character," 1851.

[6] *Disc.* pp. 266 ff.

[7] In III R 10, No. 1, *a* and *b*. He translated them in *Disc.* pp. 281 ff.

[8] Translated by Smith, *Disc.* pp. 274 ff.

[9] Translated in *Disc.* pp. 269 ff.

[10] Translated in Smith, *Disc.* pp. 267 ff.

[11] This group also includes two fragments, Lay. 19, B, and Lay. 29, B: the last was translated by Smith, *Disc.* pp. 283 ff.

third group (16 lines), is made up of inscriptions which are badly mutilated; viz. Lay. 71, B, which is continued in Lay. 73, A,[12] the merest fragment.   Only about a third of the original tablet has come down to us.   Lay. 71, A is scarcely in a better condition, and is continued on the same stone by Lay. 71, B.   The two inscriptions are separated by a perpendicular line through the width of the stone, so that Lay. 71, B, line 1, is the continuation of Lay. 71, A, line 16.

There remain a few Annal Inscriptions which cannot be classified by the number of their lines: viz. III. R. 9, No. 2; a fragmentary 19 line tablet;[13] III. R. 9, No. 3, lines 22–41 (Lay. 65), a 20 line inscription;[14] the very badly broken 18 line tablet, Lay. 66;[15] III. R. 10, No. 2, consisting of the broken parts of an originally 47 line inscription,[16] and III. R. 10, No. 3, composed of 24 lines.

Schrader's second division, the *Prunkinschriften*, includes a long fragment of a tablet which was inscribed on both sides, the middle portion (about 50 lines on the obverse, and 50 on the reverse, *i.e.* about 100 in all), being missing. It was published II. R. 67; and translated by Smith,[17] Eneberg,[18] and S. Arthur Strong.[19]   The duplicate of this

---

[12] Translated by Schrader, *KAT.*[2] pp. 261 ff.; and Smith, *Disc.* pp. 282 ff.

[13] Translated by Smith, *Disc.* pp. 275 ff.; Rodwell, *RP.* V. p. 45; and Schrader, *KAT.*[2] pp. 217 ff.

[14] Translated by Smith, *Disc.* pp. 276 ff.; Menant, *Annales,* p. 146; and Rodwell, *RP.* V. pp. 46 ff.

[15] Translated by Smith, *Disc.* pp. 285 ff.

[16] Translated by Schrader, *KAT.*[2] pp. 225 ff.; Rodwell, *RP.* V. pp. 51 ff.; and by Smith, *Disc.* p. 284.

[17] *Disc.* pp. 256 ff.

[18] *Journ. Asiatique*, VI, pp. 441 ff.; cf. *KAT.*[2] p. 224, lines 23–28, and p. 257, lines 57–62.

[19] *RP.* V. pp. 115 ff.

inscription (Brit. Mus. D. T. 30) is of special interest, having been found by Smith at *Kalaḫ* in the Temple of Nimroud, and is apparently a Babylonian copy.[20] It was published by Schrader,[21] and translated by Smith.[22] Lay. 17, F, is a 36 line tablet, translated by Schrader,[23] Menant,[24] and Oppert.[25] In 1893 P. Rost supplied the need of a complete edition of all the inscriptions, with a new set of autographs, a transliteration, and translation.[26] In it he publishes for the first time three small tablets.[27] He was fortunate enough to discover a squeeze of Lay. 17/18; which was made before the tablet was broken.

To what kings these mutilated sculptures and tablets belonged was for a long time a puzzling question. Layard himself,[28] having compared them with a pavement slab of the same period and with reliefs of the Central Palace, concluded that they all belonged to the same king. After Hincks[29] had deciphered on one of the reliefs the name of Menahem, king of Israel, as a tributary to the Assyrian king in the eighth year of the latter's reign, on the basis of a reference to 2 K. xv. 19 and 20, and 1 Chr. v. 26, Layard concluded that this king must be "an immediate predecessor of Pul, Pul himself, or Tiglath Pileser." With the discovery of the Eponym Canon the possibility

[20] Rost, vol. I. p. 11.

[21] *Kong. Ak. d. Wiss.* 1879.

[22] *Disc.* pp. 254 ff.

[23] Lines 20–25 in *KGF.* p. 206, and lines 4–10 in *KGF.* p. 106.

[24] *Annales*, pp. 138 ff.

[25] *Expédition des Rois d'Assyrie*, p. 336.

[26] *Keilschrifttexte Tiglat-Pileser's III* in two volumes. All references to the inscriptions hereafter are to this work.

[27] Vol. II. p. 15, Pl. No. 24, and Kuj. Gallery, No. 66 and No. 64; also K 2469.

[28] "Disc. in Nineveh and Babylon," p. 617.

[29] *Athenæum*, June 3, 1852.

of this king being an immediate predecessor of Pul was
obviated.   But on the other hand, the difficulty was not
lightened, because Pul is mentioned in 2 K. xv. 19, as
the conqueror of Menahem, and again, together with
Tiglath Pileser in 1 Chr. v. 26.   He was not recorded
in any Assyrian inscriptions, and, of course, not in the
Eponym Canon.   It would have been easy to have ascribed the tablets to Tiglath Pileser without further
debate.   But although no name was found upon what
afterwards turned out to be the mutilated Annal Inscriptions of the king in question,[30] yet to have thus arbitrarily
assigned them to Tiglath Pileser still left the question of
the identity of Pul undecided.

George Smith[31] conjectured that Pul was, . . . "either,
Vul-Nirâri III, who might still have been reigning in 772,
or a monarch immediately succeeding Ashurdan II or
III, or that Pul and Tiglath Pileser are identical."   This
last theory had already been propounded by Sir Henry
Rawlinson,[32] and independently by R. Lepsius.[33]   It was
finally established as the correct one by Schrader.[34]   We
may add here what is the clinching proof.   In one of the
Babylonian King Lists,[35] we read, Col. iv :[36]

[30] Lay. 17 and 18, and II. R. 67 are not Annals.

[31] "The Assyr. Ep. Can.," p. 76.   Smith still placed some faith in the
Ussher Chronology, according to which Menahem began to rule in 773–
772.   Then, of course, Vul-Nirâri (Ramman-Nirâri) would have to
reign until 772.   Smith himself inclines to the identity of Pul and Tiglath
Pileser.

[32] H. Rawlinson in G. Rawlinson's Herodotus, 1862, I., p. 382; and
Athenæum, Aug. 22, 1869, p. 245.

[33] Über d. Chronologischen Werth d. Assy. Eponymen, 1869, p. 56 ; also
Schrader, KAT.² p. 227, and KGF. pp. 442 ff.

[34] KAT.² p. 227.

[35] Pinches, PSBA. May 6, 1894.

[36] Translated, Sayce in RP. New Series, I, pp. 18 and 23.

line 5. *Nâbu-šum-ukîn* his son for one month and 12 days.

line 6. The 31 (years) of the dynasty of Babylon.

line 7. *Ukin-zira* of the dynasty of Saši for three years.

line 8. *Pulu* for 2 (years).

Compare this with the Babylonian Chronicle,[87] Col. 1.[88]

line 17. For 2 months and . . . days *Šuma-ukîn* reigned over Babylon.

line 18. *Ukin-zira* seized upon the throne.

line 19. In the 3d year of *Ukin-zira*, Tiglath Pileser.

line 20. When he had descended into the country of Akkad.

line 21. Destroyed *Bît-Ammukani* and captured *Ukin-zira*.[88]

line 22. For three years *Ukin-zira* reigned over Babylon.

line 23. Tiglath Pileser sat upon the throne of Babylon. A comparison of lines 7 and 8 of the first inscription with lines 17 ff. of the second proves conclusively the identity of Tiglath Pileser and Pul, showing that the impartial Babylonian historian gave him the respective names he bore in both Assyria and Babylon.[89]

All this is in perfect accord with the entry in the Ptolemaean Canon,[40] which notes for the year 731, the year in which Tiglath Pileser was crowned in Babylon, " *Chinzirus and Porus.*" This is, of course, the *Ukin-zira* and the *Pulu* of the Babylonian King Lists; *Porus* being a Persian

[87] Winckler in *ZA*. II. 23.

[88] Th. A. 23, where the name is *Ukînzir*.

[89] Similar changes of name are the following: Shalmaneser IV and Ashurbanipal are in the Babylonian King Lists called Ululai and Kandulu respectively. For comment, see Winckler, *Geschichte*, p. 221, n.

[40] See Smith, "Assy. Eponym Canon," p. 102.

corruption of *Pul*.[41] The fact that Berosus [42] makes Pulus, "*Rex Chaldaeorum*," is in agreement with the above evidence. It simply means that Tiglath Pileser III came to the throne of Babylon only after having conquered *Ukinzira*, head of the *Bit-Amukkani*, a powerful Chaldean tribe. Finally, Schrader [43] settled for all time that all the inscriptions belong to Tiglath Pileser.

There is in all these sources of Tiglath Pileser's reign scarcely any specific reason for doubt as to the accuracy and trustworthiness of the reports which they give us. We have not, for instance, as is the case with Sargon,[44] any variant records and versions of the inscriptions; and while they are, of course, subject to such doubt as always attaches to the official records of a time which so far lacks the historical sense and the morale of the scientific historian, as to glorify a king or a nation at the expense of exact truth, still, we find no contradictory testimony in them. Even the figures in the records of captives and of tribute furnish scant reason for doubt.

If we possessed contemporaneous documents from other nations to control the official records, there could be no hesitancy in using them to check the inscriptions, but in the one instance where we do possess such a contemporaneous inscription, an inscription mentioning the name of Tiglath Pileser,[45] the latter's reports are confirmed. And this is also true of the Biblical references to him. The

---

[41] *KAT.*[2] p. 238, and Pinches, *PSBA.* 1883–84, pp. 190 ff.

[42] *Polyhistor ap. Eusb.* Chrn. I. 4.

[43] *Kritik,* pp. 10 ff. Although previously he had denied the identity of TP. and Pul, in *ZDMG.* XXV, p. 453.

[44] Olmstead, "Sargon of Assyria," p. 7.

[45] Published by Eduard Sachau, in *Mitthl. aus d. Orientalischen Sammlungen, Köng. Mus. zu Berlin,* Heft XI. p. 55.

clues given us in the Eponym Canon, the Assyrian Chronicle, the Ptolemaean Canon, the Babylonian Chronicle, and the Babylonian King Lists, refer, of course, mainly to the fixing of dates, and in the case of Tiglath Pileser at least, confirm each other, although they are independent witnesses.

The reign of Tiglath Pileser III is especially important, because with him began a new era in Assyrian history. This king prepared the way for that period of his country's progress in which Assyria attained her greatest territorial extent. Perhaps in his time it was not yet evident that Assyria was too small a nation to hold her own against the half civilized hordes which later on accomplished her downfall. The fact that Assyria remained intact long enough to establish much which has become valuable and even essential to civilization and culture is in no small degree a credit due to this great warrior, who founded a well organized Empire upon foundations which his predecessors had enfeebled, and who was a personality great enough to have dominated his day. This was so not only because the times into which he was born invited revolution and change, but because his own power as warrior, statesman, and organizer, forced even the priesthood, always a tremendous influence, to bow to his energy and will. A great pity it is that his " literary remains " fell prey not only to the ravages of time and accident, but also to the desecrating hand of one of his great successors, Esarhaddon, who wilfully mishandled the records of Tiglath Pileser and is mainly responsible for the sadly mutilated condition in which they have come down to us.

CHAPTER II

The Eponym Canon for the year 745 announces that on the 12th day of Airu, Tiglath Pileser III ascended the throne of Assyria. Because of the entry for the previous year 746, "rebellion in *Kalaḫ*," it has been assumed that his accession was due to a military revolution, and every known fact tends to corroborate that view. Certain it is that Tiglath Pileser only gained the throne because of the condition of Assyrian affairs, and not because he was the legitimate successor to the royal office. The Empire was in very deep trouble. Its prestige was at low ebb. Abroad its influence was fast waning, and at home all the elements of a vast political upheaval had for some time been steadily tending toward revolution. The land was priestridden. Its wealth swelled the coffers of the temple treasuries, and its soldiers nourishing the traditions of ancient prowess had to be content with feeding upon the memories of former national glory. There was crying need for a leader of real ability. The land was not a victim of natural impoverishment. There were means sufficient for all purposes of national aggrandizement, could but the man be found who possessed the requisite qualities of leadership, the man who could compel the greedy priesthood to relinquish its hold upon those resources which it had come to look upon as rightful and legitimate prey. The people and the army demanded a

10

sufficient portion of the national income to defray the cost of military and civil affairs.

It must have been a sad reflection for the Assyrian soldier to review the fortunes of his country for about a century before the year 745. Persistently and steadily ancient foes were encroaching upon Assyrian territory. The mother country was still intact, but on every hand the buffer states which great conquerors had been at extreme pains to erect as barriers against invasion, had thrown off the yoke; and even worse, powerful monarchs of other nations, taking advantage of the lethargy which had come over Assyria, were conquering lesser peoples and building empires which in their new greatness boded ill for Assyria's future. Since 860, when Shalmaneser II ascended the throne, lasting and effective victory was seldom with Assyria, although royal scribes, courtier-like, record a number of military triumphs. With the exception of Ramman-Nirâri III (810–782), no able, vigorous king had ruled. That king reigned over a vast empire which stretched from the borders of Elam on the south, to *Na'iri* and *Andia* in the north, and as far as the Mediterranean on the east.[1] He was warlike, and only one of his reign years, the eleventh, was spent at home. Four campaigns against *Hubûskia*, and six expeditions to the East, are a proof of the energy which Assyria, under him, was exerting in its efforts for conquest. Even against the successor of Hazael of Damascus, who had conquered and probably ruled over Israel, Ammon, and Philistia, he ventured to war and probably took Damascus.[2] But dur-

---

[1] *Die sogenannte synchronistische Geschichte* in *KB.*[1] pp. 194 ff. is to be assigned to Ramman-Nirâri III; cf. Winckler, *Untersuchungen*, III. p. 25.

[2] *Steinplatteninschrift aus Kalah*, in *KB.*[1] I. pp. 189 ff., lines 5–12.

ing his reign he was stoutly opposed by the growing power of Urarṭu. Menuas of Urarṭu took from Assyria the tribes around Lake Urumia, and annexed large parts of Hubûskia, erecting on the rocks of Rowandiz Pass the steles which record his achievements.[3] He drove the Assyrians from Lake Van,[4] and got as far East as beyond the Euphrates, levying taxes on Miletene.[5] His son Argistis continued the work of his mighty father,[6] and from at least one passage of his Annals,[7] we must conclude that he defeated the Assyrians in a great battle. The year 778 in the Chronological Lists[8] records a campaign against Urarṭu. This is the defeat suffered by Shalmaneser at Sarisadas.[9] The years 776 and 774 both record Urarṭian campaigns, in both of which Assyria lost ground.[10] Thus Assyria, under the feeble rule of Shalmaneser, lost her northern possessions and those of Miletene. In 773 and 772,[11] in order to hold the West, campaigns had to be undertaken against Damascus and Ḥadrak, the former of which had been thoroughly subdued by Ramman-Nirâri III. There must also have been disturbances in Syria, for the land of Patin of Ashurbanipal has already in the time of Tiglath Pileser III become split up into the four principalities of Unqi, Sam'al, Yaudi, and Patin. Also against Ḥatarika, which had become the dominant power

---

[3] Scheil and de Morgan, Stèle de Kelichen, in Recueil de Travaux, Vol. XIV. pp. 153 ff.

[4] "Inscription of Palu," Sayce, CIV. JRAS. vol. XIV. pp. 558 ff.

[5] Op. cit. JRAS. XXIX, A and B.

[6] "Annals of Argistis," op. cit. pp. 572–582.

[7] Op. cit. pp. 558 ff.

[8] Cf. KB.[1] pp. 210–211, entry for the years 766 and 755.

[9] "Annals of Argistis," JRAS. XXIX. p. 693.

[10] Op. cit. pp. 602–609.

[11] KB.[1] pp. 210–211.

in Northern Syria, Ashurdan had twice to wage war,[12] while in 754 he was engaged with Arpad, which together with *Hatarika* had come to share supremacy in Northern Syria. Thus it will be seen that Assyria was gradually losing its grip, and the revolt recorded for 746 in Kalah, which resulted in the enthroning of Tiglath Pileser III, by showing the feebleness of his predecessors, only emphasized the weakness which had come over Assyria. Now there was need of a great man, a need which was supplied in the person of the soldier who, whatever his real name was, seized the reins of government and began his rule, assuming the name of one of Assyria's greatest conquerors, and becoming Tiglath Pileser III.

The fact that he gained the crown raised the uprising to the dignified status of a revolution; and it was certainly anti-priestly in its essential character. So much is evident from the history of his successors, from Shalmaneser to Esarhaddon. As long as the tribute of dependencies was available for military purposes, so long the imposition of the temple taxes by the priesthood caused no appreciable fiscal difficulties. Once this source of income became curtailed, the immense revenues of the priesthood must have loomed large in the eyes of all divisions of secular society. And these revenues were exempt from the ordinary uses of the state. The larger cities (these were of priestly origin) also enjoyed such privileged exemptions that an anti-priestly movement would be sure to arouse antagonism from them. Hence a successful revolution certainly did not receive its inspiration from them. For the country population, however, and those interested in them, it would provide relief. Upon them the burden of taxes fell with

[12] *KB.*[1] pp. 210–213.

impoverishing force as soon as the stream of tribute ceased
to flow into the imperial coffers. This state of affairs
found in Tiglath Pileser the man who knew how to take
advantage of the situation.[13]

His son had in the nature of things to follow the policy
of his father. But, whereas the former could rest his demand for popular approbation upon the success of his
military exploits, and did not have to support his reputa-
tion for anti-priestly feelings on an exaggerated repression
of the priesthood, his son, lacking the glamour of military
achievements, could only prove his loyalty to the forces
which had crowned his father and himself by consistent
antagonism to the priests and the priestly cities. He
went so far as to levy tribute upon the sacred city of
Ashur.[14] The statement that Ashur in his anger[15] gave
the throne of Shalmaneser to Sargon can only mean that
the priestly party, profiting by the feelings of revulsion
which this sacrilege must have caused, regained sufficient
power to overthrow the military party. How basic the
conflict between priest and people was can be determined
from the actions of the subsequent kings, Sennacherib,
Esarhaddon, and Ashurbanipal. The first once again
favored the military party,[16] and the last followed in his
footsteps, while Esarhaddon, like Sargon, never failed to
exalt the hierarchy. The affiliations of Tiglath Pileser
III are amply evidenced when we compare his attitude
towards Babylon with that of the two last named kings.

[13] Cf. Peiser, *Skizze der Babylonischen Gesellschaft*, in *Mittheilungen
d. Vorderasiatischen Gesellschaft*, 1896, Heft IV. s. 162–163.

[14] K. in Winckler's *Sammlungen*, II, 1, and translation in *Forsch*. I.
pp. 403 ff.

[15] *Op. cit.* 34 ff.

[16] *KB.*[1] p. 121.

He was as hostile as they were favorable. Esarhaddon indeed showed his feelings by an act unique in Assyrian history. In providing materials for the building of his palace at *Kalah*, he purposely mutilated and then removed the sculptures and tablets of Tiglath Pileser from the Central Palace of Shalmaneser II.

About the ancestry of Tiglath Pileser III we know little. But despite the fact that he was a usurper, which may only mean that he was a younger son and not in the direct line of succession,[17] there is no need to assume that he was not of royal blood.[18] In truth he never mentions his father. But that proves little, for the same is true of Sennacherib, whose relationship to Sargon we know only from the words of Esarhaddon.[19] Nor does Esarhaddon's desecration of the Central Palace monuments compel us to deny royal lineage to the usurper. As we have seen, this can be reasonably explained as Esarhaddon's protest against the actions of an "impious" king. In fact, there is good reason to believe that he was the son of Adad-Nirâri IV.[20]

[17] See also Tiele, *Geschichte*, p. 226.

[18] Rost, vol. I. p. viii, n. 1, makes the scribe (*Ann.* 31 and *Th. A.* 26) merely a flatterer who manufactures a royal ancestry for TP. Such a view is unnecessary, and, I believe, incorrect. The reference to *Ann.* 31 is a mistake.

[19] *KB.*² p. 125, lines 3 and 4, and Prisms A and C.

[20] *Forsch.* Band II, 1905, pp. 356 ff. The usual succession of the kings preceding TP. is as follows (cf. Tiele, *Geschichte*, p. 206); Ramman-Nirâri III (811–783); Shalmaneser III (782–773); Ashurdan II (772–755); Ashur-Nirâri (754–746). A glance at the Chronological List fully justifies this order. But two facts are to be noted in connection with it. First, the line between the years 764 and 763 in the Eponym Canon. The presence of this line was usually explained by the notice for 763, "In the month of Sivan an eclipse." But this explanation will not serve, since in all other cases such a line is only found between the beginning of one reign and the close of a preceding one. Secondly, the years

The personality of the new ruler can only be drawn in
meagre outline. We have no evidence by means of which
to characterize him, further than to say in the most general way that he was brilliant and energetic as a military
leader, and that his natural endowments as a statesman
were fully equal to the demands of the circumstances
surrounding him.   That he was far-sighted, his policy
of colonization, which we discuss elsewhere, proves. He
seems to have set a new fashion quite remarkable for an
ancient conqueror, in that no indication of wanton cruelty
can be cited from the inscriptions. As with his successors,
Sargon and Esarhaddon, torture and wholesale slaughter
are limited to occasions where such actions arose out of
imperative need. Nor can he be justly charged with mere
lust for conquest. As an usurper he had of course to
make good his position.   But his continuous campaigning, with its accompanying exploitation of foreign territory, and the imposition of enormous tribute, arose out
of the needs of the Empire when he came to the throne.
If he had to make extensive conquests for any other reason

763, 762, 761, 760, and 759 all record revolts.   Only with 758 does this
state of affairs end with " Peace in the land." Added to this an Armenian inscription (see Belck and Lehmann, *Berl. Ak.* 1900, p. 118) calls
Ashur-Nirâri (the immediate predecessor of TP.) the son of Adad-Nirâri.
Was this Adad-Nirâri III (810–781)? That is not likely; for, in that
case, Ashur-Nirâri (754–746) began to rule twenty-seven years after his
father, and we would have to assume that Shalmaneser III, Ashurdan III, and Ashur-Nirâri II were brothers. In other words, three suc-
cessive kings were brothers. Certainly an unique occurrence. Winckler's
reconstruction of the succession is probably true to all the facts. The
line between 764 and 763, as do all similar lines in the Canon, denotes
the succession of a new king. The Armenian Inscription referred to
calls Ashur-Nirâri the son of Adad-Nirâri. Since this cannot be Adad-
Nirâri III (812–783), we must postulate for the year 763 a king, Adad-
Nirâri IV, who ruled until 754.

than to enlarge the Empire, it was only to secure a steady inflow of tribute with which to relieve the burdened financial condition of the people. Only in that way could he verify the contention of the revolutionists, that the current poverty was due to the unreasonable exactions of the priesthood. Had the mere lust of conquest animated him, he would have been an usurper of only the common Oriental type. An examination of the records strongly militates against such a conclusion. While the Assyrian chronologists, not being historians in the modern sense, tell us nothing of the circumstances leading to the revolution, we are enabled to infer the truth of the situation from one very significant fact. The first care of an ordinary usurper is to secure himself against the claims and operations of the legitimate heir whom he has displaced. In the case of Tiglath Pileser III, the party of the natural heir was the priesthood. Had the demand for a complete change not been nation-wide, he could not have ventured to leave his capital shortly after his coronation. Hardly had six months elapsed, however, *i.e.* in the first half of his first regnal year,[21] when he went forth upon his initial campaign. No merely usurping adventurer would have dared to risk such a move.

[21] Rost, vol. I. p. XI. Since he came to the throne after but two months had elapsed, he reckoned 745 as his first regnal year. As a rule the "*reš šarruti*" denoted the first full calendar year of a king's reign.

CHAPTER III

From the very first it was evident that Tiglath Pileser had formulated plans to meet the problems which faced him and his country. So far as mere conquest was concerned many of his predecessors had been eminently successful. It was only when the question of organizing conquered territory and peoples had arisen that they had failed. Up to Tiglath's Pileser's time, conquest and revolt succeeded one another with almost unfailing regularity, and the length of time during which most dependencies remained loyal was in direct proportion to the military capacity of the then ruling king. Tiglath Pileser planned to make an end of such opportunist allegiance. He inaugurated a system of colonization designed to make of the Assyrian Empire a well-regulated and organic whole, whose farthest possessions would be firmly united with the imperial country by organic ties. In this respect Tiglath Pileser was an innovator; but in the general plan of conquest which former kings pursued he could well afford to be an imitator. They had followed a perfectly natural and reasonable course. The practical aim of all these monarchs was identical; viz., on the south Babylon was to be held as a dependent vassal, and on the east the tribes which had colonized in Babylonia had to be restrained, lest, obtaining a permanent

18

foothold there, they might prove a serious obstacle to Assyrian expansion in that direction.   In the north the people of Urarṭu and their natural allies had to be weakened by the constant embarrassment of battle, lest by an alliance with the Armenians they should finally displace Assyria as mistress of the "**Four Quarters of the World.**"   The large stretch of territory on the west which reached to the Mediterranean contained no single nation sufficiently powerful to threaten the domination of Assyria, but the peoples settled in that region were rich in many products required by Assyria.   In the imperial plan these western lands were destined to furnish a field for territorial expansion, to provide the means necessary to keep Assyrian finances abreast of its great needs, and to supply the country with the desired commodities of import.   In full accord with this traditional plan Tiglath Pileser III undertakes his first campaign against Babylonia, setting out in September 745.   But to think that he moved against Babylon as an enemy[1] is to miss entirely the statesmanlike insight which he displayed throughout his reign. Assyria was the suzerain of Babylon; and it is very probable that Nabunâçir, the Babylonian king, seeing that an energetic man of ability now ruled at *Kalaḥ*, was glad to be able to invoke his aid against the Arameans and the Chaldeans who were threatening the eastern and southern borders of Babylonia.   Tiglath Pileser's prompt response to the appeal was not only animated by

[1] So Rost, vol. I. p. XIII.   Tiele also shares this view; cf. *Geschichte*, pp. 217 ff.   Against it are Winckler, *Hist.* pp. 113 ff., and Hommel, *Geschichte*, pp. 651 ff.   Rost's claim that TP. took the title of "*King of Sumer and Akkad*" from the beginning, does not prove that he went to Babylon as an enemy.   Assyrian suzerainty over Babylon is sufficient to account for his assumption of the title.

the need of checking these tribes, but also by personal
and political considerations. He was king by right of
revolution, but no religious consecration had legitimized
his accession. In Assyria he could not stoop to receive
such consecration, for the priesthood would not have
accorded it, and the military classes, whose antagonism
to the priesthood had fathered the revolution, would
not have condoned him had he accepted it. To them it
would have appeared that he had secretly compounded
with the Temple interests; but from the Babylonian
priesthood, whose consecration made his rule just as valid
as that of the priests of Assyria, he could and did receive
religious sanction. Nor would they withhold it provided
he consented to come to the aid of their king and country,
threatened as it was by powerful foes on the frontier.
Under their auspices he could offer sacrifices to Bel, Nebo,
Nergal (*Th. A.* 11 and 12), to Çarpanit and Tašmit, in
those Babylonian cities which he visited during his first
campaign. Then he could return home as a king whose
coronation had lost the last vestige of illegitimacy because the gods had accepted his offerings and granted him
victory.

It would also for another reason have served no profit-
able purpose for Tiglath Pileser to play the rôle of enemy
against Babylon at this time. In his first campaign a
usurper must be victorious. Had he gone forth as the
avowed enemy of Babylon in this campaign, he could not
have claimed a complete victory, unless he had succeeded in
dethroning Nabunâçir. Doubtless he could have done so,
for Nabunâçir was in no position to offer effective resistance, but such a step would have caused Tiglath Pileser
great embarrassment. To make his coronation legitimate,

he would then have been compelled to "grasp the hands of Bel." This, as we shall see below, he was unable to do at this time, and to have omitted that ceremony would have spelled a capital offence against the priesthood of Babylon. At home he could afford to antagonize the priesthood, but he could not risk a similar policy in Babylon. Unlike their compeers in the north, the Babylonian priests were at this time normally powerful in the political affairs of their country. Their influence was also strongly felt in Assyria. The Assyrians, although they had very recently participated in a revolution against their own priesthood, had no feeling of antipathy to the priests of Babylon. On the contrary, the religious influence of Babylon over Assyria was never really enfeebled during the entire period of Assyrian supremacy. It was very strong at this time. Had Tiglath Pileser crowned himself king of Babylon without "grasping the hands of Bel," he would not only have been looked upon as a sacrilegious despot by the people of the South, but also by his own countrymen, and he would have earned the enmity of a proud vassal state whose sense of independence was strong in addition to the opposition of a large part of Assyrian society. If on the other hand, in 745, he had submitted to priestly coronation, he might have gained power and popularity at home and in the South, but such added popularity would have been short-lived, especially in Babylonia, for the ceremony of "grasping the hands of Bel" had to be repeated annually in the city of Babylon. To have missed it only once would have invalidated his sovereignty. Had he attempted despite the omission to retain the crown, the feelings of the priesthood and of all Babylonians would have been outraged, and in their eyes Tiglath Pileser would have ranked as a ruthless tyrant trampling the rights and cherished convictions of his subjects under foot. He would have provided for himself a tireless enemy at his very gates and endangered his great plans. In the years to come all his campaigns would have to be arranged with a view to being present in Babylon for the imperative annual ceremony. A king whose future operations were already mapped out, and who in accordance with them would have to travel as far afield as Urarṭu, or even the Caspian Sea on the north and the Mediterranean on the west, had to postpone the assumption of full kingship over Babylon until such a time as his farthest provinces were enduringly bound to the Empire, and his governors and lieutenants had learned, under his own tuition, how to hold the king's possessions by the aid of the system which the crown intended to inaugurate.

His purpose in this campaign[2] was, then, not to subjugate Babylon, but to prevent its falling into the hands of the Arameans and Chaldeans. These tribes[3] were his first concern, since to leave them unmolested might at some future time have occasioned serious obstacles to the full prosecution of any distant expedition in which he might

---

[2] The account of this campaign is given in *Ann.* 1–7 (Lay. 68). Schrader, *Kritik*, on the basis of a comparison between Lay. 50 B, lines 5–6, and Lay. 67 A, line 5, assigns the campaign to the 18th and 19th palû, *i.e.* 733–732. This assignment Rost (vol. I. p. V) rightly rejects. *Ann.* 1–7 belong to 745, because the continuation of this record (Lay. 34 B) tells of the conquest of *Dur-Kurigalzu* and *Sippar*, which (cf. *Ann.* 12) occurred in the first palû or regnal year.

[3] *Th. A.* 5–9 mentions all these tribes. Also Sargon, Prism, I, 41–46 and V, 36–38; and Khorsabad, 18–19 (cf. 126–127) gives the following order from west to east. *Tu' Ru-bu', Ḫa-ri-lum, Kal-(?)-du-du, Ḫum-ra-nu, U-bu-lum, Rûa, Li'-(ta)-ta-ai ša a-aḫ Su-rap-pi Uk-ni-i, Gam-bu-u, Ḫi-in-da-ru, Pu-qu-du.* For *Rûa*, Glaser (*Skizze*, 189) thinks of "*Riu*." Cf. Gen. xi. 19.

happen to be engaged; and it is conceivable that while he was in the far West they might even seriously threaten Assyria. Later on he had to wage strenuous war with the Chaldeans, and their power is shown by the fact that, even when he did get an opportunity to devote his undivided attention to them, they were strong enough to hold *Šapia*, their capital, against every exertion of Tiglath Pileser, although at that time (733) his troops were veterans, and he a mighty conqueror with a long record of brilliant victories.

Now, in 745, these Aramean and Chaldean tribes had come within striking distance of Babylon. A branch of these two tribes on the east of the Tigris was nomadic, but the most dangerous although not the more numerous sections had possessed themselves of several important cities on the right bank of the Euphrates, any one of which might be used as a base of operations for an attack upon Babylon. That city once in their hands, they would have been in a position to threaten Assyria itself. Marching directly south, Tiglath Pileser attacks and takes in order the cities which were held by his enemies. These were (cf. *Ann.* 12 ff. and *Th. A.* 11), *Dur-Kurigalzu*,[4] *Sippar, Pazitu, Paḫḫaz, Nippur, Babylon, Borsippa*,[5] *Kutu*,[6] *Kiš*,[7] *Dilbat*, and *Uruk*.[8] He drove the Aramean

---

[4] Ruins of Akar-Kûf; so *Paradies*, pp. 207 f. But more probably Til-Nimrud, west of Bagdad on the Nahr Ifa, where Sir H. Rawlinson found a brick marked "*Dur Kurigalzu*."

[5] Barsip. Its god was Nebo and his temple was called *E-zida*. The Talmud (Ab. Zar. XI. b) reads, "*Beth N'bo d'Bursi*."

[6] Cf. *Paradies*, p. 217. The ruins of Til-Ibrahim a little west of Babylon. The location is made certain by the reference in the Nabuna'id Chronicle, Col. III. 10 f.

[7] J. Jensen, *ZA.* XV. pp. 211 ff., in a very painstaking investigation, distinguishes three different cities named *Kiš*. One in the extreme south

tribes from the banks of the Lower Zab to the banks of
the *Uknu* River.[9] He redug the Patti-Canal, and on the

of Babylonia. This cannot be the city mentioned for the year 745, since
in the campaign of that year TP. went no farther south than *Nippur*. A
second *Kiš* lay in northern Babylonia near Bagdad, east of the Euphrates.
A third *Kiš* is always mentioned as a neighboring city of *Ḥarsagkalama*,
in a hill district on the road between Assur and Babylon. Its name is
always written *Kiš* or *Ki-šu*. Which of the two last named cities is the
Kiš captured by TP. ? I think we may eliminate the *Kiš* near Bagdad.
Had TP. conquered two cities named *Kiš*, he would have distinguished
between them. That he dealt with the one near *Ḥarsagkalama* we may
confidently assume, because at *Ḥarsagkalama* (cf. Pl. I. 16) he offered
sacrifices to Nergal. II. R. 50, 13, mentions a temple at that place. *Ḥarsagkalama* means, "*mount of the land*." Thus *Ḥarsagkalama*, and its
near by city *Kiš*, lay in a hilly district. Since there are no hills between
the Tigris and the Euphrates, it is, I think, evident that we must look for
the *Kiš* we are seeking east of the Tigris. If this be correct, then the
Kiš placed by Winckler (*Hist.* map) between the Tigris and the Euphrates
is not the city which TP. took. And again, if our *Kiš* lay east of the
Tigris, then TP., marching south from *Kalaḥ*, got as far south as Nippur,
and returning north from there, crossed the Tigris, and, while homeward
bound, took *Kiš* and *Ḥarsagkalama*. This explains why he, after review-
ing (Pl. I. 16) the accomplishments of the campaign, sacrificed at *Ḥarsagkalama*. It was the last city he took, hence he there celebrated his
victory over the conquered tribes by offerings to the gods.

[8] *i.e. Warka ;* cf. Jensen, *ZA.* XV. 211.

[9] When the *Uknu* is mentioned with the Tigris and the *Surapi* it is
always in the following order: Tigris, *Surapi*, *Uknu*. This order points
from west to east. But if, as has been proved (*Paradies*, p. 195), the
Uknu is the modern Kercha, then the question arises what modern river
is the same as the ancient *Surapi ?* For there is no river between the
Tigris and the Kercha. Delitzsch thinks of a canal corresponding to the
modern Umm-el-Jemel. But this canal is west of the Tigris, and the order
should then be: *Surapi*, Tigris, *Uknu*. The probable solution (cf. Billerbeck, *Mitthl. Vorderas. Gesellschaft*, 1898, pp. 81 f.) is that the course
of the Tigris has changed since Assyrian times. Its course then corre-
sponded to that of the Shatt-el-Hai, and what was then known as the
Surapi is our present lower Tigris, which was the channel into which
poured the various small rivers rising in the Pushti-Kuh, and which
pursued the course of the modern Shatt-el 'Arab to the Persian Gulf.
De Goeje, *ZDMG.* vol. **XXXIX**. p. 8, thinks that the *Uknu* may be the
Sura Canal.

site of " *Til-Kamri* which is called *Ḥumut* " he built a fortified city, to which he gave the name *Kar-Aššur;* also a second city the name of which was written at the end of *Annals*, line 21, but which has been broken away. Rost thinks it may have been *Dur-Tukulti-apil-išarra*. These two cities became the central garrison-posts of the conquered districts, where he settled his lieutenants, having put the territory under the jurisdiction of the two neighboring provinces of *Barḫazia* and *Mazamua*.[10] The lieutenants had not only to raise sufficient revenues for the purposes of military occupation, but had also to deliver a considerable sum to the imperial treasury, since their annual assessment was fixed at the large sum of ten talents of gold and one thousand talents of silver, besides tribute in cattle and other goods. From *E-sagila*, *E-zida*, and *E-šitlam* the priests brought gifts [11] as tokens of their submission to the conqueror.

With the completion of his first conquest Tiglath Pileser began to put into practice his policy of colonization. The conquered peoples were scattered and their lands repeopled with colonists from *Mazamua* and *Barḫazia*. His object was of course to obviate future opportunities for conspiracy

[10] Rost, vol. I. p. 7, n. 1. A comparison of line 50 of the *Annals of Shalm. II*, with his Monolith Inscription, Col. II, 75, shows that the country was interchangeably called *Mazamua* and *Zamua ;* its capital was probably *Zamri* (cf. *Annals of Asrh. II.* 61, 62). Rost (vol. I. p. 5) translates, "*Ba-ar-ḫa-zi-ia, pan piḥat (mât) Ma-za-mu-a*" (*Ann.* 17), " *der Provinz Barhaza, Mazamua*." Billerbeck (*Sulm.* p. 72) leaves out the comma between the two names, and taking them together makes of them the designation of a district in *Mazamua*, called *Barḫazia*. TP. felt himself secure in the possession of this district from the very beginning of his reign, since he annexed the conquered territory to it. It must, therefore, have been situated near the Assyrian border.

[11] The bringing of *riḥati* = ' gifts ' (Rost, p. 127), not only symbolized submission, but was in itself a priestly sanction of TP.'s coronation.

or revolution, and he rendered the subjugated tribes impotent, both by garrisoning their land and by scattering them in widely different colonies, thereby preventing the possibility of concerted action on their part.

But, although in this campaign he penetrated as far as *Nippur* in the south and had subjugated the country all the way to the foothills of Elam, clearing the plains and river basins of hostile tribes, his work would eventually have gone for nought, had he not penetrated to the hill-tribes in their mountain fastnesses in the country beyond. To have left these unmolested must have invalidated his exertions in the lowlands. From the highlands an unconquered enemy could have descended into the plains to undo all the victorious results of the first campaign.

To make Assyria secure, and to settle matters on his immediate southern frontier and his eastern borders, he undertook in the following year (744) his second expedition, that against Namri.[12]

However, the southern frontier could not be considered safe until the passes east of the Diala had been secured. Their occupation and fortification would serve the double purpose of a defensive border outpost, and in case of any future advance into the country beyond, the roads would be clear for any invasion he might contemplate. Not only is it probable that Tiglath Pileser divided his army into two corps for this campaign, but in all likelihood one of these corps moved in at least two columns. One corps

---

[12] *Namri* used to be read " *Zimri* " (cf. Smith, " Assyrian Canon," p. 64). Misled by this reading, Delitzsch (*Paradies*, p. 237) refers to the Zimri of Jer. xxv. 25. Rost (vol. I. p. xvi. n. 1) believes that the designation *Namri* may have been a general term for " East." This would be due to a popular etymology which derived *Namri* from *namâru*, 'to be or to become light, to shine,' and is probably incorrect.

operated to the south. Starting from a point not far north of modern Bakuba, it followed a course generally parallel to the east bank of the Diala and presumably crossed the divide where one of the branches of the Konchitum River breaks through the hills, not far from modern Imam-Esker; proceeding east they overran *Erinziaŝu*,[13] *Bit-Ḫamban*, *Bit-Sumurzu*,[14] *Bit-Barrua*, *Bit-Zualzaŝ*, and then *Ariarma*,[15] *Tarŝarranihu*, and *Saksukni*.

The northern corps under the provincial governor Aŝŝur-danin-ani, had the task of subjugating the "mighty Medes." They succeeded in conquering so extensive a territory that it is more than probable that they operated in at least two separate columns. But the *Annals* give us little aid in tracing their respective routes. It is probable, however, that they did not divide forces until they had reached the plain of the Shehrizor. This, so far as the nature of the country is concerned, they could have entered most easily by marching along the west bank of the

---

[13] This locality is to be sought northwest of Kizilrobat. After conquering the three countries, *Erinziaŝu*, *Bit-Ḫamban*, and *Bit-Sumurzu*, TP. could write (*Ann.* 49): "*I smote them to the borders of Assur.*" His aim was to control the mountain passes of these countries. They gave access to the more distant East, and prepared the way for the campaign of 737, "to Media."

[14] In the *Annals*, *Bit-Sumurzu* is mentioned alone. In the other inscriptions, it is always coupled with *Bit-Barrua*, the country which was immediately to the north of it, and which lay in the neighborhood of the modern Kamiran. Streck, *ZA.* XV. p. 325, locates *Bit-Ḫamban* east of the Diala between Bakuba and Mendeli. This is surely too far south. It was probably north of Kizilrobat in the vicinity of Saripul, in the hill country through which the boundary line between Suleimania and the southern part of Ardelan runs.

[15] *Ariarma, Tarŝarranihu*, and *Saksukni* are mentioned in that order in *Ann.* 56 and *Th. A*, 31. *Bit-Sumurzu* (together with *Bustus*) correspond to modern Azerbaijan; and *Ariarma*, which is mentioned after *Bustus* in Pl. II. 22, is to be located in Southern Azerbaijan and Northern Ardelan, and *Tarŝarranihu* and *Saksukni* in Southwestern Khamseh.

Diala, south of the Segrime Dagh, and continuing parallel
to the Shirwan, a branch of the Diala. At some point
which commanded the various roads into Media, perhaps
near modern Behistun, they separated. One division,
going northwest, overran *Bit-Abdadani*[16] and *Bit-Zatti*,
then turning to the northeast, on the right flank of their
former route, they defeated the troops of *Bit-Tazzaki*.[17]
The second division, starting in the direction of the southeast, overcame *Bit-Ištar*, and thence going south, carried
its victorious arms through *Bit-Sangibutti*[18] and *Bit-Sangi*.
A half turn round towards the north brought them to *Bit-
Kapsi* and finally still further north to *Araziaš* and *Parsua*.[19] The two divisions had together traced an almost
complete circle, and now probably reunited their forces at
the appointed rendezvous. Most likely this was their
point of departure near Behistun. Here it seems was the
site of *Nikur*,[20] the fortress which in *Annals* 28 was recorded as having been destroyed. It was rebuilt as a

[16] The Ramman-Nirâri Inscription from *Kalaḫ* (*KB.*[1] p. 191, lines 8–9)
reads, *Mu-un-a Par-su-a Al-lab-ri-a Ab-da-da-na Na-'-ri ana pat gim-
ri-šu.* A comparison with a passage in Sargon (*Annals*, Botta, 73, 7),
which reads, "*Al-lab-ri-a Ma-an-na-ai Ur-ar-ṭu*," shows that *Allabria*
was situated between *Parsua* and *Mannai* to the east of Lake Urimia,
and *Abdadana* east of *Allabria*, perhaps in the district around Kuh-
Karawal.

[17] *Bit-Tazzaki* and *Bit-Kapsi* are Median districts (*Ann.* 26 and
Th. A. 29 f. 34 f.), stretching from eastern *Mazamua* northward to Lake
Urumia. Their location will depend on the location of *Zakruti*, with
which they are twice mentioned (*Th. A.* 30, 36 and Pl. I. 18). If *Zakruti*
was, as is probable, in the vicinity of the Pundsch-Ali, then *Bit-Kapsi*
lay between it and the Talvantu-Dagh.

[18] East of modern Sinna.

[19] East and southeast of Lake Urumia. Together with *Bustus* it covered modern Azerbaijan.

[20] Near Behistuan. The reading is not certain; it may be "*Sal-lat.*"
Cf. Br. pp. 231 and 309.

strategic base, to control the whole country which had been overrun by both corps. Here a large number of people from the various conquered tribes were settled and a provincial governor was placed over them, while others from the north were colonized in *Bit-Sumurzu* and *Bit-Hamban*, and still others in *Zakruti*. Before arriving at *Nikur*, the two corps had effected a junction, possibly in *Araziaš*,[21] which they may have conquered together. Whether *Arakuttu*[22] and *Nisai* were also reached in this year cannot be determined.[23] Neither is mentioned in the *Annals*. More probably their turn did not come until 737, when a second war was waged in the regions here considered.

The booty yield of the campaign must have been enormous. Horses, mules, large and small cattle, camels, weapons, precious metals and stones, and all manner of

[21] Rost's emendation for *Arazi*. Location probably just west of Divandere ; cf. *Sulm*. p. 34.

[22] Fr. Lenormant (*Sur la campagne de Tiglath Phalazar II dans l'Ariane*, in *ZA*. 1870, pp. 48 ff. and 69-71) thinks that the presence of such names as *Nisai, Arakutti, Ariarma*, and *Zakruti* shows that TP. penetrated into Ariana and Arachosia. But Delattre (*Le Peuple et la Langue des Mèdes*, pp. 85 f.) has disproved that hypothesis. Rost (vol. I. p. vi. n. 1) suggests that since TP. did not penetrate into farther Media, the presence of the names may be due to the fact that some Iranian tribes did at one time press westward, and then later, because of numerous migrations of different races into Media, they returned to the East. TP.'s claim to have conquered these tribes bearing Iranian names, may be only the record of a tribute which they were forced to pay him temporarily.

[23] The following places mentioned in this campaign are not recorded in any other Assyrian inscriptions : *Šanaštiku, Ḫaršu, Ḫarsai, Kiškitara, Aiubak, Tutašdi, Kušianaš*. The lines, *Ann*. 51-58, are not meant to convey the idea that the cities and princes recorded in them were overcome after the fall of *Bit-Ḫamban*. They are a summary of the results of the campaign (lines 26-50), and are not to be regarded as chronological ; *i.e.* the cities and lands mentioned are all to be sought in any of the lands conquered during 744.

products were carried away as trophies and as profit. A tribute of 300 talents of "*uknû* stone" (lapis lazuli) and 500 talents of silver [24] was imposed, and 65,000 prisoners were deported for colonization in other dependencies.

The nearest foes were now helpless. At the end of two years' reign enough tribute and booty must have been brought into Assyria to satisfy even a people whose previous supply for some years had been a minimum. Tiglath Pileser had undoubtedly made his position so strong that for the future his campaigns might carry him to great distances without his having to fear that any revolution at home would seriously threaten his crown. These first two expeditions had proved brilliantly successful. The usurper had justified all prophecies as to his powers. Whole districts were in ashes. Old fortified towns, which had become a menace, were destroyed. Powerful enemies had been terrified by the sight of heaps of their slain and wounded, and were taught to understand what the future held in store for Assyria's foes. At important points Tiglath Pileser had erected ' *çalam šarrûtia*,' 'images of my royalty.' Much booty was dedicated to the god Aššur, and his terror was ever before the eyes of the smitten peoples (*Th. A.* 40).

Although not all the conquered districts were formally incorporated into the Empire, Tiglath Pileser had, in 744, begun the real work of assimilation and amalgamation. These eastern tribes were mostly Iranian and Kassite. The last had at one time established a dynasty of thirty-six kings in Babylon,[25] and as late as 702, Sennacherib[26] had

[24] *Ann.* 53 is broken ; but surely the tribute could not have amounted to five hundred talents of gold.

[25] Cf. Winckler, *Hist.* pp. 72 f.

[26] Tiele, *Geschichte*, p. 287.

found it necessary to suppress them. Their traditions must have made them cherish a degree of independence so strong that it proved well-nigh impossible to subdue them entirely. Perhaps it was because of this close cherishing of their independent Babylonian identity that Tiglath Pileser's plan of colonization never really resulted in their full assimilation, and they may have been the cause of his campaign of 737.

CHAPTER IV

SYRIA AND THE WEST

The object of the campaign of 743 did not contemplate direct conflict with Urarṭu[1] itself. The day for such a vital move was not yet at hand. The triumph over Median foes, although decisive, was in no way to be compared with the struggle which Sardurri III of Urarṭu was prepared to wage for supremacy in Asia. He was a foe worthy of the utmost consideration; nor would he and his people fight the less furiously and bitterly against Assyria, because the gage of the coming battle was not some petty principality, but overlordship of the whole of the northern half of the continent or perhaps independence itself. There was not room for two great powers of equal strength and resources in Asia. Great nations had not yet learned how to live amicably side by side. Between them there was sure to be constant conflict until one or the other was either thoroughly subjugated and rendered dependent upon its conqueror or was altogether annihilated. To be less powerful than a neighboring people was in itself a prophecy that independence would be shortlived.

As the situation now stood in Asia, either Assyria or Urarṭu must expect to bow to the superior prowess of the

[1] Urarṭu is the Assyrian form. The great god of the nation was *Haldiš*, and the name Haldean is sometimes used; cf. Olmstead, "Sargon of Assyria," p. 36, n. 30. C. F. Lehmann has shown (*Verhandlungen der Berliner Anthropologischen Gesellschaft*, 1900, pp. 34 ff.), that the Haldeans are the *Chaldoi* of the Greek and Byzantine writers; not to be confused with the *Kaldi*-Chaldeans.

other, and the issue might hinge upon the result of a single engagement. Nor was that issue at all a foregone conclusion. Assyria's glorious tradition was a valuable asset in the struggle to come, but this great tradition was not by any means her only weapon. As has been seen, when Tiglath Pileser III came to the throne, Assyria was in a state of lethargy, but her fundamental vitality and vigor were not impaired. It only needed a vigorous, able ruler, with whom the majority of the nation should be in full accord, to arouse her to great endeavor. That Tiglath Pileser was such a man his two previous campaigns clearly indicated; but the Urartian, too, had become accustomed to victory, and not only over petty nations, but over Assyria itself. As we saw in Chapter II, from the time of Ramman-Nirâri III, up to the very date of Tiglath Pileser's coronation, Urartian power had been steadily increasing. Menuas had measured strength with Assyria, and both he and his son Argistis had proved themselves the most aggressive and successful monarchs of their dynasty. Tiele[2] has made a list of the most important of the possessions of Menuas, and it includes the land of the Hittites, Melitene, Man, and Urmedi. He in his turn bequeathed to his successor, Sardurri III, an empire the largest part of which had been wrested from Assyria, and had been among her most valuable possessions. When Tiglath Pileser came into contact with Sardurri, Urartian territory had attained its widest extent. Its northern and northeastern boundary line ran through the Plains of Alexandrapal[3] and Gokcha Lake (Transcaucasia)

[2] *Geschichte*, p. 215 ; cf. also Sayce, *CIV*. XXXVII–XLIV.

[3] See C. F. Lehmann, *Verhandlungen der Berliner Anthropologischen Gesellschaft*, 1900, p. 33. No account of Urartian history, geography, and culture can afford to overlook the work of Belck and Lehmann. Most of it has been published in the journal referred to.

and stretched on the northwest to Hassankala near Erzerum, Aschgerd, and Delibaba. On the west was the Murad Tschai, with the furthest outposts at Masgerd north of Kharput, and at Isoli. On the south its line ran along the mountain range between Armenia and Mesopotamia, and on the extreme east, from Gokcha Lake to Ordaklu. Nor does this large empire seem to have hung together loosely. The manner in which many of the independent states resisted Tiglath Pileser proves that the Urarṭian kings had succeeded to a surprising degree in rendering vassals and tributaries firm in their fidelity. The determined and bitter opposition which the Syrian princes offered to the arms of Tiglath Pileser, compelling him to spend three years in the West before they could be forced to forswear their adherence to Sardurri, indicates the large measure of Urarṭian mastery over very wide territorial possessions.

Sardurri had also shown his capacity for military accomplishments. By the year 755 he had conquered Melitene,[4] and by 744 the countries of Taurus and Amanus were also his. Upon these and the support of Arpad he could depend in the contest now before him. It is indeed a matter of wonder that he did not press on to the further West and conquer both Damascus and Israel. The first was at this time very weak, and Israel, though apparently prosperous during the reign of Jeroboam II, was, as Amos testifies, not inherently strong. The weakness of neighboring kingdoms fully accounts for the outward glory of Jeroboam's reign; and even this was beginning to fade during the last years of his life.[5] Perhaps Sardurri realized that it was impolitic to attempt further extension of

---

[4] Cf Inscriptions of Isoglu, Sayce, *JRAS.* XVI, pp. 642 ff.
[5] Cf. Hosea, i, ii, iii.

territory at this time, because Tiglath Pileser had shown
that he was no weakling. It would suffice the Urartian
king for the time being, if he could only hold his own
against Assyria. Nor was it any part of his plan to push
further west away from his home provinces, and leave
a strong enemy in his rear. He could afford to let the
Assyrian make the first move. This, Tiglath Pileser was
compelled to do. Perhaps one of the secret wishes he
entertained in making his campaign of the previous year
in Armenia and the East was that Sardurri would leave
Van and come south to meet him on neutral ground.
But Sardurri did not stir. To have attempted to march
against Sardurri's capital[6] and strike at the very centre
of things would have meant a long trying journey through
snow-bound mountain passes, easy for the Armenian to
defend. For a hazardous attempt of that kind Tiglath
Pileser was not prepared in 744. He dared not risk the
chance of a reverse. In that case the Urartian allies
would have clung all the closer to their allegiance, and it
was with these allies, particularly with the Hittites and
Syrians, that much of Sardurri's power lay.

The most promising plan, therefore, was to strike some-
where in Northern Syria. The tribute and taxes from
this rich part of Asia were essential to Sardurri, and their
threatened loss would not fail to bring him from his
mountain-guarded capital into the plains. Here without
incurring the danger, fatigue, and delay of a long march
around Lake Van, the advantage was with Tiglath Pileser.
Should Sardurri stay at home, he would be the loser,
since that must have amounted to a confession of fear,

---

[6] The name of the capital was Turušpa. It is the classical Thospites.
For the various forms of the name, see Sayce, *JRAS.* 1882.

and as such have been a moral blow at the influence of Urarṭu.

The sources mention [7] *Agûsi*,[8] *Qummuḫ*, *Melid*, *Sam'al*,[9] and *Gargum*, as the active allies with whom Tiglath Pileser had to deal. Early in 743 he marched west, and the Canon entry for that year [10] reads, "*ina Arpadda*," in the city of Arpad. Nowhere in his inscriptions does Tiglath Pileser hint of a battle or a siege which secured to him the possession of the city in this year. There is no justification, with Rost,[11] to change the preposition from, "*ina*," to "*ana*," and on that basis postulate a situation wherein Tiglath Pileser besieges that city and was forced to raise the siege when he heard that Sardurri was coming to the relief of his ally. The Canon distinctly reads, "*Ina Arpadda*." But we do not know how he entered and took possession of it. Tiele [12] thinks that in 744 Arpad was in possession of Assyria, and that Tiglath Pileser meant to use it in this campaign as a base of operations. At any rate, although we do not know how Tiglath Pileser entered the city, for it was the capital of Mati'ilu, the strongest ally of Sardurri, we are forced to admit the fact. While there preparing for operations against the surrounding small states, the news of Sar-

---

[7] *Ann.* 60–63.   *Th. A.* 45–46.

[8] *Bit-Agûsi*, Schrader, *KGF.* p. 207, n.   The capital was Arpad (Tel-Erfad, between Aleppo and Azaz).   From Shalm. II, Monolith II. 24–30 and 82–84, it must be located between the Afrin and the Euphrates, *i.e.* with *Patin* on the west and *Bît-Adini* beyond the Euphrates on the east.

[9] Its capital was probably at *Zinjirli*, where the Bar-Rekûb inscriptions were found.

[10] *KB.*[1] p. 212.

[11] Vol. I. p. XII, n. 2.

[12] *Geschichte*, p. 219.

durri's approach was announced. From the northeast the Armenian came through *Kilḫi* and *Ulluba*, across the Tigris, and then east of the Euphrates into *Qummuḫ*. He had reached a point between *Kištan* and *Ḫalpi* when Tiglath Pileser appeared, and the rivals joined battle between the two cities.[13] Sardurri sustained a bad defeat. He fled the field on the back of a mare.[14] His loss was 72,900 men (*Annals* 66). His baggage-train, horses, mules, chariots, even his personal ornaments, became the spoil of the victor; and the servants and skilled workmen who had followed the army were made captives. Yet despite all this the battle was not decisive. A single victory had not decided the fate of the West, nor was Sardurri entirely helpless. The picture of a complete triumph with which the Annals would impress us is not the full story. The victory must have cost Tiglath Pileser much of his strength. He was compelled to return to Nineveh and prepare his forces for another campaign in Syria. The allies were not intimidated because of Tiglath Pileser's victory. He found them even more difficult to overcome than Sardurri himself; and this is es-

---

[13] Rost, vol. I. pp. XVIII ff. thinks that TP., believing that the proximity of Arpad, which according to him was still in Sardurri's power, was no place for the battle, crossed the Euphrates south of Til-Barsip, to reach *Kištan* and *Ḫalpi*. After the battle TP. pursued Sardurri to the Euphrates north of *Amid*, and destroyed *Ezzida*. This cannot be correct. In this campaign TP. does not mention crossing the Euphrates before the battle of *Ḫalpi*, and to have raided in *Ulluba* (as Rost believes) would have necessitated the crossing of the Tigris, which he would not have failed to mention had it taken place. What TP. really did was to cross the Euphrates at the " Bridge " (*Ann.* 68) after the battle ; then he raided *Ezzida*.

[14] *Annals of Sargon*, II. 107. This was considered a subject for ridicule ; cf. Belck and Lehmann, *Verhandlungen der Berliner Gesellschaft*, 1896, p. 325.

pecially true of Mati'ilu of *Agûsi*.[15]   It was he who made
Tiglath Pileser spend three years in Northern Syria,
prosecuting secondary campaigns, but principally en-
deavoring to reduce the city of Arpad.   We have seen
that the Canon for 743 records the entrance of Tiglath
Pileser into Arpad.   The year 742 tells of another expedition against the same city; likewise the entry for 741,
adding that it took three years to capture Arpad.   As has
been said, in 743 Tiglath Pileser left Arpad to meet Sardurri in *Qummuḫ*.   Thus, if that city only surrendered
to the Assyrian king in 741, it appears that while Tiglath
Pileser was engaged in *Kištan*, the allies in Syria took
Arpad during his absence.   And the great king, exhausted by the all-day battle in *Qummuḫ*,[16] could do
nothing more in 743 than capture a few cities in that
land.   *Ezzida*,[17] *Ḫarbisina*, and *Ququsanšu*, he sacked after
crossing the Euphrates.

[15] This opinion of Tiele is justified by Lehmann, *op. cit.*, 1896, p. 324.

[16] *I.e. Kommagene*, Schrader, *KGF*. pp. 129 ff.

[17] *Pl*. I. 34, puts *Ezzida* in *mât Enzi*.   To locate the three cities in the
text we must first locate *Enzi*.   Schrader, *KGF*. pp. 129 ff., comparing
Shalm. II, Monolith. 92–93, with Lay. 47, 28–33, makes the river *Arsanias* = the modern Murad Su.   He notes (p. 144) that Šamši-Ramman's
(Col. II. 10–12) marching route brings him to *Enzi*, and that he can
cross the *Arsanias* only after traversing that land.   *Enzi* thus lies in the
mountainous district between the Euphrates and the Tigris (upper and
western) and the Murad Su.   Streck, *ZA*. XIII, p. 94, equates *Enzi* with
the modern Hanzeth, between Palu and Arghane, and identifies it with
Alzi (Shalm. II, Monolith. 42, 45, 46).   *Enzi* was an Urarṭian province,
but Streck's identification is not correct.   It is not the same as *Alzi*.
Enzi bordered on *Alzi* (*Alzis* of the *CIV*.; so Sayce, *JRAS*. XIV. p. 398).
It lay between Palu and Khini, *i.e.* east of Lake Van, between the
Euphrates and the Murad Su.   *Pl*. I. 33, says that *mât Enzi* borders on
Qummuḫ.   There *Ezzida* and the other cities of *Enzi* must be sought,
east of the Euphrates and southwest of the Murad Su.

Rost, vol. I. p. **XX**, makes *Ezzida*, *Ḫarbisina*, and *Ququsanšu* cities
of *Ulluba* (*Kilḫi*); but, p. **XXVII**, he says they are cities around " upper

While Tiglath Pileser was wintering in Nineveh preparing for a resumption of operations in Syria in the following year, Mati'ilu made ready for the inevitable siege of Arpad. He would have made his peace with Tiglath Pileser, and had he done so, it is probable that he would have received reasonable terms. But Sardurri had escaped into his own land, and his ally expected him to gather a new force with which to come to the help of the beleagured confederates in Syria. When therefore the Assyrian again appeared before Arpad he faced a very sturdy opposition. How well Arpad must have prepared for this siege is evident from the time it required to take the city. Certainly Tiglath Pileser did not sit down idly before the walls and quietly await the starvation of the city. Expeditions from his armed camp were sent out in all directions and the allies were carefully watched, in order to prevent concerted action. When in 740 the city at last capitulated, all the members of the league save one were anxious to compound with the victor. The fate of Mati'ilu was sealed. He lost his throne, and were the records complete, we should undoubtedly hear of his execution. Uriarik of Que,[18] Pisiris of *Karkamiš*,[19]

Nairi Sea," *i.e.* Lake Van. These cities were all east of the Euphrates (*Pl.* I. 33-36). The battle with Sardurri was fought in *Qummuḫ*, which was bounded on the east by the Euphrates; *i.e.* the battle was fought west of that river.

[18] Western part of Kilika, from Amanus to Taurus, in the northwest; cf. Schrader, *KFG*. pp. 236 ff.

[19] The general location is obtainable from Shalm. Monolith. I. pp. 29 ff. His route from east to west is *Adini, Qummuḫ, Gargum, Sama'l, Gargamiš, Patin*. It was the capital of *Ḫatti* (Tiglath Pileser I. col. V, 49; *alu Gargamiš, ša māt Ḫa-at-ti*). It is to be located in the ruins of Girbas, on the right bank of the Euphrates near Birejik. Cf. *Paradies*, pp. 265 ff.

Kuštaspi of *Qummuḫ*, and Tarḫulara of *Gargum* [20] hurried
to Arpad in person to make peace with Tiglath Pileser
and acknowledge his overlordship.   The terms he exacted
were heavy.   The *Annals*, wherein the amount of tribute
was stated, are broken (*Annals* 89–90) ; all that remains is
the mention of ivory, elephant skin, purple cloth, lead,
silver, and gold.   But the measure of their humiliation
was complete, and they had no desire to prolong resistance.
Had they seen fit to do so, a new leader would have proclaimed himself in the person of Tutamu of *Unqi*. [21] *Unqi*,
originally only the western edge of *Patin*, had at this
time gained control of the whole country. [22]   It lay between the Euphrates and the Orontes rivers, and stretched
north beyond the Afrin.   The capital city was *Kinalia*,
and against it Tiglath Pileser proceeded without delay.
From a passage in Asurb. III. 70–92, [23] we may determine
the route which the army followed.   They started from
a point between *Karkemiš* and Til-Barsip and had to
cross the Afrin before reaching *Kinalia*.   But they first
reach Hazzaz ('Azaz).   This being an important city,
there was probably a military road from *Karkemiš* and
Hazzaz, which led to the Afrin River.   In later (pre-
Grecian) times, such a road went from Birejik (Zeugma),
a little south of the site of *Karkemiš* to Aintab.   After
capturing Hazzaz (*Kl.* II. 27), Tiglath Pileser dealt
similarly with *Aribua* (*Kl.* II. 27), and continuing south
struck the road which comes up from Aleppo, runs a

[20] Southwest of *Sama'l*, between the Pyramos and the Sadshur rivers.

[21] *Unqi* = '*Amk*; cf. Tomkins, "Bab. and Orient. Record," vol. III. p. 6.

[22] From 812–740 the records are meagre ; during that time the subjugation of *Patin* by *Unqi* took place.

[23] The passage is translated in Winckler, *Forsch*. 1893, pp. 3 ff. and
KB.[2] 106–111.

little south of Hazzaz, and thence through the Syrian Gates to Beilan and the coast. He came to *Kinalia* after following this road across the Afrin,[24] and took it without much difficulty. In the course of the attack it was destroyed. This we must infer because in *Annals* 97 we are told that it was rebuilt. *Unqi* was placed under a provincial governor, and much booty compensated for the expense and trouble of the campaign. Tutamu forfeited his life. His fate was a dire warning to all neighboring princes, and it was lucky for Hiram of Tyre and Rezin of Damascus that their emissaries had been hastened to Tiglath Pileser with tokens of submission shortly after he had reduced Arpad.[25]

Tiglath Pileser was not yet finished in the far West, but it will perhaps be better for us, for the time being, to disregard the chronological order of his campaigns, and leave his activities in *Ulluba* (739), and the expeditions against Media (737), and *Mt. Nal* (736), and that against Urarṭu (735), for other chapters, and to continue here the details of his work against Syria, Phœnicia, Philistia, Israel, and Judah, which occupied him in 738, and again from 734 to 732 inclusive.

The principal countries of the West which remained independent of Assyria after Tiglath Pileser's campaign of 740, were Syria, Israel and Judah, Phœnicia and Philistia. With these in his possession the Assyrian king would have been supreme from the Tigris to the Mediter-

---

[24] *Kinalia* must therefore be located in southern '*Amk*.

[25] There is some dispute as to the date of *Ann.* 77–89. Hommel refers them to 734, but Rost has assigned them to 740. This is in all probability correct, because the Syrian princes had no occasion to swear allegiance to TP. in 739, after the *Ulluba* campaign or, in 736, after the expedition to Mt. Nal.

ranean Sea.   Perhaps he had originally intended to devote
the year 739 to the subjugation of these countries and the
reduction of the entire West.   But during that year
trouble broke out among the Nairi peoples and a campaign
had to be undertaken against *Ulluba*.   The uprising in
that country was probably incited by Sardurri.   Seeing
that Tiglath Pileser was rapidly becoming master of the
West, the king of Urarṭu fomented trouble in Ulluba,
hoping thereby to compel his Assyrian rival to hurry back
to the East and thus give the western kings an opportunity to form a league against their conqueror.   In this
Sardurri was more than successful.   Princes and principalities which had been subdued in 740 rebelled against
the Assyrian yoke.   Thus when the work of 739 in Ulluba was completed Tiglath Pileser naturally prepared for
a second western campaign, and accordingly in 738 we
find him once again in Syria.   Up to this year Sardurri's
plan of fomenting rebellions against Tiglath Pileser in
one part of Asia while the latter was busy in another, had
been successful.   While the Assyrian king was engaged
in the West, rebellions inspired by the Urarṭian monarch
broke out in the East.   And when Tiglath Pileser hurried
East to crush them, Sardurri incited revolts in the West.
It was because of this fact, as we have seen, that Tiglath
Pileser was compelled to operate in Ulluba in 739, instead
of devoting that year to a continuation of the Syrian campaigns of 740.   But Tiglath Pileser was too great a conqueror to be long diverted from his great purpose by such
machinations.   With Ulluba conquered he was only one
step nearer to his ultimate goal; viz., the conquest of
Urarṭu.   Nor did Sardurri gain much by the formation
of the new league of western kings with which Tiglath

Pileser had to deal in 738. For the latter defeated the western confederacy, and when he was ready to come to a final accounting with Sardurri, it was no longer necessary for him to do preliminary work in *Ulluba*, since that country was already his.

For the Syrian campaign of 738 the Canon makes the objective point *Kullani*.[26] Its ruler probably played an important part in the uprising, but the real leader was Azriau[27] of *Yaudi*.[28] *Yaudi* had been governed by the

[26] *I.e.* Kalneh ; cf. Is. x. 9, and Amos vi. 2, between Arpad and Hamath.

[27] The identity of *Az-ri-ia-au* of *Yaudi* is a matter of dispute. Among those who think he is identical with Azariah of Judah, are Schrader, *KGF.* pp. 395 ff. and *KAT.*[2] pp. 217 ff., and Hommel, *Geschichte*, pp. 662-663. Oppert, *La Chronique Biblique fixée par les eclipses, des inscriptions cunéiformes*, 1867, pp. 30 ff. and *Solomon et ses successeurs*, 1877, pp. 1-23, makes him a son of Tabeel (Is. vii. 6). Winckler, *Forsch.* vol. I. pp. 1 ff., presents a series of arguments which put an entirely new face upon the matter. He argues that the king in question cannot be Azariah of Judah. In 733-732, Ahaz, king of Judah, was with TP. in Arpad. But TP.'s campaign against Azariah took place in 738, so that the years between 734 and 738 must suffice for the end of Azariah's reign and also for the full and independent reign of Jotham. Although the chronology of Kings is admittedly artificial, yet the sixteen years ascribed to Jotham (2 K. xv. 33) indicate a fairly long reign. The attempt to get over the difficulty by assigning the fourteen years' difference as a portion of his rule contemporaneous with Azariah, would make him king in 738. And why is not Jotham, but only Azariah, mentioned in TP.? Then, too, what is Azariah doing so far north? *Ann.* 125-132 gives a list of the XIX districts of Hamath which conspired with Azariah against Assyria, and all of them lay between the Mediterranean and the Orontes, north of Lebanon. Winckler would solve all difficulties by identifying the *Yaudi* of the TP. Inscriptions with a country of the same name mentioned in the *Zinjirli* Inscriptions (*Ausgrabungen* in *Sendschirli*; in *Mittl. aus d. Orientalischen Sammlungen, Köng. Mus. zu Berlin*, Heft XI, 1893), and this certainly clears up the puzzles concerning the possibility of Azariah's taking the field in 739, and of his influence in the far north. Rost (*Ann.* 105 and 123) reads " *Izriau*," and suggests that this reading may decide the question. The change of initials from " A " to " I " he notes also in the names *Iskaluna*; *Askaluna*. The text of 2 K. xiv. 28, which has been

house of Panammu of *Sam'al*, and undoubtedly under that
dynasty had, as a result of the conquest of Arpad, become
attached to Assyria.   Now that a new coalition, independent of Urarṭian leadership, proposed to contest supremacy
with Tiglath Pileser, the kingship of Azriau, who was not
of the house of Panammu, points to the overthrow of the
pro-Assyrian party in *Yaudi*.   The confederacy, including the "XIX districts of Hamath," was made up of
cities [28] and states situated between the Mediterranean and
the Orontes north of Lebanon.   It is not probable that Israel or Damascus was actively involved in this uprising,
although it is somewhat surprising that Rezin was not the
prime mover.   He had begun about this time to make himself felt in Northeastern Syria, and was certainly the most
powerful monarch in that part of the country.   His resources were ample for a determined· conflict, as he proved
in 732.   Now, he and Menahem [30] of Israel hasten to render
tribute as soon as the news of Azriau's defeat reached them,
and all the confederated kings swore fidelity to the great
conqueror.   *Qummuḫ*,   *Tyre*,   Que,[31]   *Gebal*,[32]   *Karkemiš*,

relied upon to prove a close connection between Hamath and Israel, is too
corrupt to prove much (cf. Benzinger, *Könige*, 1899, pp. 166 ff.).   TP.
mentions *Az-ri-ia-au* only in reference to North Syrian campaigns, so that
the king and his land must be sought in that part of the country.

[28] East of *'Amk*, north of Antioch, and west of the Afrin ; therefore
between *Unqi* and *Sam'al*.

[29] Its cities, *Ḫuzzara, Tai, Tarmanazai, Kulmadara, Ḫatatirra*, and
Sagillu, are only mentioned in TP.'s Inscriptions.   Some of these can be
located with certainty ; *Arqa*, now the ruins of Til-Arka, south of Nahr
el Kebir.   *Çimirra* (Gen. x. 18) is now Sumra.   It commanded the passage from the coast to the upper Orontes valley ; cf. *Paradies*, p. 282.

[30] 2 K. xv. 19, 20, records an invasion of Pul ; but the *Annals* are
silent as to this ; it may be that a small force under a lieutenant visited
Samaria.

[31] Its capital was *Tarzi* ; *i.e.* Tarsus.

[32] Now Jebeil.

Hamath,[33] *Sam'al, Gurgum, Melid, Kask, Tabal,*[34] *Atun, Tuḫan, Iśtunda,* and *Ḫuśimna,* and even the land of an Arabian queen, Zabibi, became vassals of Assyria. The tribute they were obliged to render included money, precious metals, wood, cloth, camels, horses, and herds of cattle. The booty was so large that it seems as though Tiglath Pileser's object was not only to reimburse himself for the cost of the campaign, but also to make Middle and North Syria too poor to dream of the possibility of revolt for years to come. With that end in view he also colonized the territory with settlers from Western Media, where, while he was occupied with the Syrian league, a rebellion had arisen. Sardurri, unable to face the Assyrian king on the open field, sought to hamper him by diplomacy and intrigue ; for doubtless the uprising among the Median tribes in this year was due to Urarṭian influence. But if Sardurri thought that Tiglath Pileser would hurry east and leave the allies in Syria free to throw off the yoke, he miscalculated. Tiglath Pileser did indeed find himself compelled to leave Syria after crushing the rebellion, and to postpone the conquest of South Syria, Israel, and Judah, and the Lebanon region until another time ; and he had in 737 to proceed against Media itself. But he was able to deal with Azriau and his allies in 738, and subdue them so thoroughly that, when four years later

[33] Cf. *Paradies*, p. 275. Its capital was *Amat.*

[34] Tabal in Ez. xxvii. 13, xxxii. 26, xxxviii. 2, xxxix. 1, always with Meshech ; it lay north of the upper Euphrates, and west of Erzingun. The relative location can be ascertained from Sargon, Cyln. 15 (*KB.*[2] p. 40) ; from east to west he places *Bît-Ḥamban, Parsua, Mân, Urarṭu, Kasku, Tabal, Muski ;* on the east *Tabal* bordered on Kikilia ; cf. Esarh. Cyln. II, 10–13. "*Nisi (mâtu) Ḫi-lak-ka (mâtu) Du-'u-a a-śi-bu-ut ḫur-śa-ni śa di-ḫi (mâtu) Tabal.*"

he traversed their lands, *en route* to Damascus, they were harmless to harass him.   The revolt on the Babylonian border was soon checked by the governors of *Nairi* and *Lullumi*,[35] who sent about 25,000 prisoners to Tiglath Pileser.   He settled them in the cities of *Unqi*, and then had thousands of the Hittites scattered throughout the *Nairi* lands.

For three years there was peace in the West.   On the surface of things, all the princes who had sworn allegiance to Tiglath Pileser continued faithful, and he, satisfied that further operations in that direction could wait until Sardurri had been reckoned with, did not return until 734. For that year, according to the Canon, Philistia was the objective point.   But it would have been strange if the real trouble had not proceeded from another quarter.   In 738 Rezin had hurried to placate Tiglath Pileser with gifts.[36]   But, as has been observed, Damascus was a power-

[35] An inscription of one of the kings of this country has come down to us.   It is in double columns and was copied by de Morgan (de Morgan and Scheil, *Recueil*, XIV. pp. 100 ff. 1891).   The name occurs also in the form *Lullubi*.

[36] The tribute list for 738 includes North and Middle Syrian rulers; viz., Hamath, Samaria, Phœnicia, *i.e.* Tyre, and *Gubal*.   In that of 734 Damascus is missing, but new names occur; viz., Armad (modern Island of Ruad; cf. Gen. x. 18), Ammon, Moab, Askalon, Judah, Edom, Gaza. Both lists have *Sam'al*.   As a contemporaneous document mentioning TP.'s name, the inscription of Bar-Rekûb of *Sam'al* is worth quoting (cf. Winckler, *Vorderasiatische Gesellschaft*, 1896, p. 198):

1. I Bar-Rekûb,
2. Son of Panammu king of *Sam'al*,
3. Servant of Tiglath Pileser the lord of the
4. Four quarters of the earth, because of the righteousness of my father and because
5. of my righteousness, my lord Rekûb-el seated me
6. and my lord Tiglath Pileser on
7. the throne of my fathers. . . .

Bar-Rekûb erected his monument in *Yaudi* instead of *Sam'al*, where we

ful state. Its position among the Middle and South Syrian kingdoms was a leading one, and some of its earlier rulers had proved their power, even in conflict with Assyria itself. Ramman-Nirâri, despite his boastful language,[87] had found its king Mari[88] a strong foe; and now in 734 Rezin[89] had again succeeded in making his kingdom of Damascus a state to be reckoned with. No doubt Tiglath Pileser had his eyes fixed on the countries beyond Damascus, including Palestine. It is also almost certain that this great king had planned a future conquest of Egypt. Damascus was the real obstacle in his way. Cappadocia and Que on the north shore of the Gulf of Iskanderun were his; so was Syria south of Damascus, and

should have expected to find it, perhaps because TP. after the events of 738, gave part of *Yaudi* to a house of whose loyalty he was sure. It is surprising that a vassal should express his loyalty so sincerely. The Biblical references express no such sentiment. A reason may be found in the following: In Shalm. Monolith. II. 42, the land is (*mâtu*) *Sam'al*. No further mention of the land occurs until TP. In his *Annals*, 152, and in *Th. R.* 8, it is (*alu*) *Sam'al*. Perhaps in the course of the incessant fighting between the neighboring states, *Sam'al* had, in the interval between Shalm. II and TP., been constantly worsted and had found that in loyalty to TP. lay its only safety. Probably this loyalty was not so much to Assyria as to TP. himself. A great statesman like TP. understands how to attach a vassal to his person. A glance at the Eponym Canon for 681 may convince us. Here *Sam'al* is recorded for the first time since TP.'s death. Now, however, it is an Eponym and not a member of the house of Panammu who governs *Sam'al*. In that year Esarh. came to the throne. That he dishonored the memory of TP. we know. Perhaps because the house of Panammu was loyal to TP.'s memory, Esarh., who treated political foes with the utmost leniency, was sufficiently displeased to end the career of the line of Panammu, and to incorporate *Sam'al* into the empire, placing a governor at its head.

[87] Cf. *KB.*[1] p. 191, lines 14 ff.

[88] Perhaps this is the Biblical Ben Hadad III ; cf. Kittel, *Geschichte*, vol. II, p. 250, n. 5.

[89] This was Rezin II. The first was a contemporary of Solomon, 1 K. ii. 23.

even that together with Israel was already nominally in his hands, but since Mati'ilu of Arpad had opposed him for three years, Rezin was prepared to do no less. Why the Canon makes the principal goal of this year's expedition Philistia [40] we do not know. The mutilated condition of the *Annals* for the two succeeding years compel us to go to the Biblical sources for a picture of the operations which follow.

The record of Menahem's tribute (2 K. xv. 19, 20) is the point of departure. This king came to the throne as a result of anarchy in Israel (2 K. xv. 23). His short reign was unsettled; and his successor, Pekahiah, was murdered by Pekah, the captain of the palace guard (2 K. xv. 29). Anarchy in the north gave Judah her long-expected opportunity.[41] Alone, in her troubled state, Israel was in no position to cope with her southern opponent. She had to invoke outside help, and the logical ally was Damascus. Pekah called Rezin to his aid, and the two together laid siege to Jerusalem. Ahaz, who had only recently come to the throne of Judah, did not know whither to turn for succor. Isaiah's advice he rejected.[42] The enemies without the gate had to be repulsed. Nor did they seem to Ahaz to be as insignificant as " two tails of a smoking firebrand." Of what good was it to him that before many years the riches of Damascus and

---

[40] Schrader, *KGF*. p. 125, believes that " (*mât*) *Pilištu* " stands for a general designation of the East ; *i.e.* Philistia and Israel. Rost, vol. I. p. XXIX. n., is inclined to doubt this very much, since the entries opposite the Canon dates seem always to state the goal of a campaign. But there is no way to reconcile such a claim with the positive fact that TP. was, in 734, mainly engaged with Damascus, and that Philistine operations were only incidental to the main campaign.

[41] Judah desired revenge for Israel's victory at Beth Shemesh (2 K. iv. 11).   [42] Is. vii. 1 ff.

Israel would (Is. viii. 4) "be carried away before the eyes of the king of Assyria"? And of what use was faith in God while Pekah was hammering away at the gates? "The waters of Shiloh that go slowly" (Is. viii. 6) were not quenching the firebrands. It became imperative to enlist help from some quarter, and there were but two possibilities, — Egypt or Assyria. Of these two, Assyria was the logical ally, because Israel had traditionally made alliance with Egypt (Hos. viii. 12). Ahaz appealed to Tiglath Pileser, since from him he could expect more consideration than from Pharaoh. "I am thy servant and thy son; come up and save me out of the hands of the king of Syria and out of the hands of the king of Israel" (2 K. xvi. 7). No second invitation was needed. Menahem had already paid tribute, but now Tiglath Pileser had an excuse to overrun the country. He came, but had no need to proceed against Samaria or against Damascus as yet. Ahaz had invoked his aid, but the Assyrian had his own plans. *En route* to Jerusalem there were other lands to conquer. Moreover, Rezin and Pekah went each his own way; the one to Samaria, the other to Damascus.

Probably taking the usual route through the Lebanon depression in the Orontes valley, Tiglath Pileser made several Phœnician cities tributary, and an expedition into Philistia under one of his generals succeeded in subduing that land. Hanno of Gaza, not daring to resist and unwilling to surrender, fled to Egypt.[43] We may see from this

[43] The Muçri (*Kl.* I. 1, 9) referred to here cannot be an Arabian or an Idumean people, despite Winckler's suggestive contention, in *Untersuchungen*, pp. 168 ff., and *Mitteilungen des Vorderasiatische Gesellschaft*, vols. I and IV, "*Muçri, Melucha und Ma'in.*" We must remember that Egypt was the only power strong enough to dispute Assyria's progress

circumstance that the eye of Egypt was upon current events. Egypt was never safe without outposts in Syria and never failed, when possible, to secure and hold these. Tiglath Pileser was working his way rapidly into the zone where every advance step must have caused apprehension to the Pharaoh. The latter probably had promised aid to Hanno, as he had often done with Israel and Judah; for it was very necessary for him to keep a buffer between himself and Assyria, but he failed to keep his promise. Gaza's independence was important to Egypt, for it was the nearest city on the trade route between Egypt and Syria, and controlled this route. With Hanno a fugitive, Gaza fell into Tiglath Pileser's hands. He now proceeded to deal with Pekah. On the western borders of Israel (2 K. xv. 29), "The king of Assyria took Ijon, and Abel-beth-maacah, and Janoah and Kedesh and Hazor and Gilead and Galilee and all the land of Naphthali, and he carried them captives into Assyria."[44] Pekah must have resisted valiantly, and the losses of Israel would doubtless have been greater but for the presence of a pro-Assyrian party. Pekah's folly in allying himself with Rezin and thus becoming the indirect cause of Assyrian

at this time. It was, therefore, to Pharaoh that Hanno fled. Without the prospect of Egyptian aid, he would have followed the course of his neighbors and have paid tribute to TP. Pharaoh did not actually help him until 726, for in that year we find him in the field against Sargon.

[44] *Kl.* I. lines 6–18. The text is badly mutilated. In line 6, Rost fills out, *Gal(za)*. To fill out the lacuna after " *Gal*," it has been proposed to read *Ga-al-lil*, *i.e.* "Galilee"; that would agree with the text of 2 K. Schrader, after the second " (*alu*) " in the line reads, *Abel-beth-Ma-khah*, which again would agree with Kings; but Rost correctly insists upon the reading, *A-bi-il-ak-k(a)*. The gap at the beginning of line 7, which precedes . . . *li*, Hommel fills out with (*Nap-ta*)-*li*, *i.e.* Naphthali: again with geographical justification only.

intervention, probably accounts for his murder [45] (2 K. xv. 30). The new king, Hosea, certainly the leader of the pro-Assyrian party, was allowed by Tiglath Pileser to retain his throne as a tributary. That he swore fidelity to Assyria we see from 2 K. xvii. 3, 4. There we are told that Shalmaneser "found conspiracy" in him, . . . "for he had sent messengers to So, king of Egypt."

Tiglath Pileser was now free to deal with Damascus. Assyria and Syria had met on the battle-field in past times, and both had registered victories, but Rezin seems to have lacked both the ability and the prudence of his predecessors. It is not clear why he separated from Pekah instead of remaining with him to face the common foe. Perhaps Rezin feared that should the battle take place in Israel, Tiglath Pileser had a sufficient force to send troops against Damascus while he himself was busy helping to defend Israel. Such an expedition was actually sent against Philistia, while the main army was engaged in Western Israel. Also Rezin had other allies. That he may have considered it better policy to keep Tiglath Pileser busy in Israel, west of Anti-Lebanon, and cause him to weaken his forces in fighting Pekah, so that he himself could gain time to form a new confederacy, is possible. Perhaps in his view that was a wiser course than to trust to the issue of a single battle.

The Syrian proved as difficult to overcome as Sardurri, but the latter at least saved his capital. Rezin after a long siege had to surrender his royal city, but not until his outlying dominion was ravaged from one end to the other, and its cities, towns, and hamlets sacked. Rezin

---

[45] *Ann.* 228, and *Kl.* I. 17. TP. tells only of Pekah's flight, not of his death.

himself suffered death.[46]   The inhabitants of Damascus
were transplanted to Kir.[47]   The districts which were conquered in 732 were placed under a provincial governor
with his residence at Damascus.

Metena of Tyre,[48] and Mitinti of Askalon, who had
formed the new coalition with Rezin, lost heavily in tribute,
and the last, crazed by his misfortunes, was replaced by
his son Rukiptu, as an Assyrian vassal.   To add to the
wide extent of the conquest, an Arabian queen, Šamši, who
may have been an active ally of Rezin's, was pursued into
her home country, and after the defeat of her troops, and
the payment of heavy tribute, was allowed to keep her
throne.   Many of the Arabian tribes were made tributary,
and of these, one, the Idibi'il,[49] were stationed to guard and
control the Arabian Muçri.

Now the princes of all the West hastened to do homage to
the conqueror.   At Damascus he established a temporary
court, and from far and near came trembling rulers with

---

[46] The record of Rezin's execution is not in TP.   Rawlinson discovered
part of a tablet which recorded it, but the tablet was left in Asia and has
been lost ; cf. Schrader, *KAT.*[2] p. 265.

[47] Kir is not mentioned in TP.'s records, probably because of their fragmentary condition.   Halévy, *Récherches Bibliques*, pp. 57–58, locates it in
or near Elam, on the strength of a reference in Is. xxii. 6.   Amos i. 5 and
ix. 7 makes it an Aramean city.

[48] The terror with which Tiglath Pileser inspired his foes is shown by
Metena's surrender.   No city was better situated to withstand a siege
than Tyre, and TP. could not have taken it without a fleet, any more
than he was able to conquer Turušpa later on.

[49] Cf. *Paradies*, pp. 301 ff.   They were a tribe situated north of the
Dead Sea, toward the Egyptian border.   Their location, near to Egypt,
might perhaps justify the belief that the Muçri of *Ann.* 226, filled into
the text by Rost, was Egypt, and their watch upon that country was the
first step taken by TP. towards an invasion of Egypt.   Of course TP. did
not live to return to the West and to undertake a campaign against
Egypt.

promises of loyalty and with "presents."[50] The booty which they were compelled to deliver was enormous. Only one prince, Uassurmi of *Tabal*, dared to absent himself, and for this presumption he had the humiliation of seeing a "nobody"[51] placed on his throne.

Assyria was now mistress of Asia, from the *Uknu* River to the Philistian coast, in the south, and on the north, from the Mediterranean to *Qummuḫ*. The East, to the Caspian, had been conquered in 736. Media had been thoroughly subdued in 737. Urartu had been rendered harmless in 735. Only the work of freeing Babylonia of the Chaldeans remained to be done. We may now proceed to review the campaigns of 737, 736, 735, 731, and 730.

[50] When the various kings came to Damascus to render tribute, Ahaz is simply mentioned among the rest, and not as an ally. A proof of the view TP. took of his call for help. The author of 2 K. xvi. 5–18, makes a side issue of the trip of Ahaz to Damascus, whither he went to swear allegiance to TP. (v. 10). His chief interest lies in the affair of the altar which Ahaz saw at Damascus, and the plans of which he sent to Urijah the priest, with orders to build a replica. Urijah obeyed, and Ahaz thought well enough of the work to set the altar in the Temple. Can it be possible that we have in this transaction a hint of one of the terms imposed by TP., upon Ahaz? For what altar did Ahaz copy? Surely not the altar of the discredited Rezin, his bitter foe. Is it possible that TP. not finding it necessary to go to Jerusalem in person, demanded that Ahaz set up an altar which would be a counterpart of the one before which the latter had sworn fealty? TP.'s custom of setting up *çalam šarrutia*, "images of my royalty," before conquered towns, will be recalled. Was the altar in question a variation of such an image?

[51] *Th. R.* 15, "*mar la-ma-ma-na.*"

CHAPTER V

MEDIA AND URARṬU

In 743, Tiglath Pileser had come into **direct conflict with** Sardurri at *Kištan* in *Qummuḫ*, and although victorious, had been so far crippled by the battle, as to prevent him from following up the Urarṭian king. During his march into *Qummuḫ* he had lost Arpad, and since that was the objective point of that year's campaign, he returned to besiege it in 742. But although Arpad remained for the time being in the hands of Mati'ilu, its rightful king, and despite the fact that Sardurri had made his escape, Tiglath Pileser was not so far exhausted by the battle of *Kištan*, but that he could cross the Euphrates and raid the cities of *Ququsanšu*, *Ḫarbisina*, and *Ezzida* (*Ann.* 77–81). However, he neither desired at the time nor was he able to press on nearer to the Urarṭian capital, and invade *Ulluba* and *Kilḫi*. Arpad had first to be taken and Northern Syria to be conquered.

But *Ulluba* and *Kilḫi* were the objective points in 739. They had to be in Assyrian hands before Sardurri could be searched out in his home land, and doubtless the work of this year was only another step towards the investment of Van, which was undertaken in 735. The particulars of the campaign are meagre, for the Annal record is missing, and the remaining inscriptions give few details.[1] The

---

[1] The sources for the campaign are, *Pl.* I. 25–29 and *Pl.* II. 41–45, and *Th. A.* 43–44. The cities mentioned cannot be located.

Canon furnishes only the bare announcement, "to *Ulluba*."[2]
In 831, Shalmaneser II had been compelled to send an expedition into *Ulluba* and *Kilḫi*, for the Urarṭians had
already at that time annexed those two countries, and they
had been under the control of Urarṭu ever since. Now in
739 Tiglath Pileser inaugurates that series of campaigns
which was designed to culminate in a final reckoning with
Sardurri, whom he had from the beginning recognized as
Assyria's most dangerous foe. If he can conquer *Ulluba*
and *Kilḫi* and so administer them as to keep them loyal, he
will not only have destroyed the buffer state which pro-
tected Urarṭu on the west, but will open a way for his
troops to Sardurri's very door. The brevity of the sources
does not give the impression that great importance was
attached to the accomplishments of the year. We are told
that a city, *Aššur-iki-ša*, was established, where the cult
of Aššur was instituted, and where a governor was installed
to administer the two conquered provinces. In *Ilimmir*
he erected an image of his royalty.[3]

The following year finds Tiglath Pileser again in the
West, and in 737 he was engaged in Media. But in 736[4]
his operations are prosecuted in nearly the same territory
which engaged his attention in 739. At the foot of the

[2] The sentence which completes the entry in the Canon, "(*maḫazu*)
Bir-tu ça b-ta-at," has caused controversy. Peiser (*KB.*[1] p. 212) translates, "*Die Stadt Birtu wird erobert.*" So also Smith ("Assyr. Canon,"
p. 65). Rost, vol. I, p. XII, n. 4, translates, *eine Festung wird gegrün-
det* : by reference to IR. 14, 17, he shows that *çabâtu* may be translated
"established." He observes that if the record dealt with the reduction
of a fortress, the Assyrians themselves would not have known which one
was meant unless a name were given.

[3] *Ilimmir*, probably a small country in the *Nal* Mountains, perhaps a
semi-dependency of *Ulluba*. The name, I think, occurs only here.

[4] The sources for the year are *Ann.* 177-190 ; and *Pl.* I. 28.

Nal[5] Range were fortresses and natural conformations which would be of great defensive value to Urarṭu should Tiglath Pileser attempt to invade it.   Furthermore, the Assyrian had to possess them in order to feel secure against a raid by Sardurri into *Ulluba*.[6]   At *Kištan* Sardurri had suffered a stinging defeat, and since then his best provinces had been taken from him.   Although he had not ventured into open conflict all the while he was being despoiled, and was seemingly content to remain quietly at home, he could not be trusted to remain a passive spectator altogether. There was no telling what sudden enterprise he might institute or at what point he might unexpectedly emerge. *Kilḫi* adjoined Urarṭu on the southwest, and it was from that direction that he could most quickly appear.   He had to gain only one victory and Tiglath Pileser would have suffered a setback perhaps sufficient to hamper his plans for years.   The Urarṭian was at all times a dangerous enemy against whom precaution was as imperative as active campaigning.   All the more therefore did Tiglath Pileser need to secure the *Nal* region.   To hold it, once *Ulluba* and *Kilḫi* were in his hands, made the conquest of these lands complete and the possession of *Nairi* final.

Tiglath Pileser took the most important cities of the

---

[5] Rost, vol. I. p. XXVII, correctly locates the range as the one stretching south of Lake Van, and separating Urarṭu on the south from northern *Ulluba* and *Kilḫi;* identical with the Armenian Taurus. Cf. also Streck, *ZA.* XIII., p. 106, who locates it more precisely.   He places *Ulluba* on the southwest of *Nal*, east of *Kirḫu*, north of Kanari, between the rivers Jezidchaneh and Bitlis-Tschai.

[6] The cities, none of which can be exactly located, are (*Ann.* 177), *Ḥista, Ḥarabisina. Barbaz, Tasa.   Ann.* 180–181: *Daikansa, Sakka, Ippa, I'linzanšu, Luqadansa, Kuda, I'lugia. Dania, Danziun, Ulai, Luqia, Abrania, I'usa. Muqania* and its capital, *Ura* (*Ann.* 183), are not mentioned in any other inscription.

district.   Ten thousand prisoners were captured, and over 20,000 head of cattle, together with a large number of mules and horses, made up the profits of the campaign. Why Tiglath Pileser did not penetrate *Ulluba* and *Kilḫi* in 739 we do not know; perhaps because of lack of time; or it may be that only a part of his army was engaged at the time while he was busy preparing for other campaigns. Perhaps, too, Sardurri, pursuing his favorite policy, fostered sedition against Assyria in Media, while Tiglath Pileser was busily engaged in the North and the East. At any rate, one of the years intervening between the campaigns of 739 and 736 was spent in the East, and the following one,[7] as the Canon has it, was devoted to " *(mât) AA.*"[8]   A part of the country subdued in this campaign

---

[7] The campaigns of 744 and 737 have been well studied by Billerbeck, *Sulm.* pp. 72 ff.   The inscriptional sources are *Ann.* 157–176, *Pl.* I. 17, *Pl.* II. 19; and *Th. A.* 29–38.

[8] Rost, vol. I. p. XXV, without hesitation, reads the " *(mât) A. A.*" of the Canon, as *Madai*, and considers it an abbreviation of *Mad-ai.*   He finds convincing confirmation for his reading in Sennacherib, Cyl. A, Col. II. 30, which reads *(mât) Ai*, while the parallel passage in K. 1674 omits the determinative *(mât)*, and simply reads, *Mad-ai.*   It can, I believe, be proved that two distinct localities bore the name *Madai.*   One of these was *Umliaš* (cf. *Br.* 11693), a land east of the *Uknu River.*   This *Umliaš* is not the land which TP. knows as Media; he distinguishes sharply between them.   *Ann.* 157–158 read, *(mât) Bit-Kapsi (mât) Bit-Sa-angi (mât) Bit-Taz-zak-ki (mât) Ma-da-ai*, i.e. *Bit-Kapsi*, etc., in *Media* ; and *(mât) Bit-Zu-al-za-aš (mât) Bit-Ma-at-ti (mât) Umliaš :* i.e. *Bit-Zualzaš*, etc., in *Umliaš.*   The lands mentioned in *Pl.* I. 18, together with *Madai*, are in Uraṭu proper or near it.   All are in the north, and so also must this *Madai* be, for *Pl.* I is arranged geographically, not chronologically.   Sargon, Prism, Col. II. 30 *(KB.*[2] pp. 89–91), mentions *Madia* with *Ḫarḫar*, which was near the Uraṭian border.   Thus we have *(mât) A. A.* in the North and one also in the South.   Certainly in this year TP. was engaged with the northern one.   Delitzsch made two attempts to locate *(mât) A. A.*, and both are seen to be correct when we remember that there were two lands so designated.   In *Paradies*, p. 247, he said it was the country around *(šad) A-ja*, in Kurdistan.   This

had been dealt with in 744.   That it had to be reconquered
does not speak well for the thoroughness of the first expedition, but does not warrant our thinking that the work
was laxly done at that time.   In the first place, Tiglath
Pileser had to contend with the machinations of Sardurri,
and no conquest could be considered final until the latter
was thoroughly routed.   As in the West and the North,
so here in the East, uprisings were undoubtedly fathered
by him.   People who would never have dreamed of throw-
ing off the yoke so soon after having experienced the
power of Assyrian arms, were incited to rebellion by
Urartian persuasion.   Then, too, the campaign of 744 was
only Tiglath Pileser's second one.   He had not yet conquered a sufficiently large number of peoples to transplant
into these Median and Elamitish districts, thus to impair
the homogeneity of the original population.   There were
still enough of the native inhabitants left to allow of concerted action.   It must also be remembered that in 744
Tiglath Pileser's possessions were not yet extensive, and
he had not sufficient land in which to scatter conquered
tribes.   Hence the work of 744 had to be repeated.[9]   The
sphere of operations as located by Billerbeck (*Sulm.*
p. 85) was in the valley of the Derund, about Sinna, the
territory between the Pendsch-Ali and Talvantu-dagh,
and also in the vicinity of Sakkis.   Whether, as in the
first campaign in this region, the army moved in one or
more corps, is not to be decided, for we have no hint as to

is the North Media.   In *Assyr. Gram.* p. 18, he equated (*māt*) *A. A.* with
Umliaš.
      [9] The names which occur both in this campaign and in that of 744 are
Bit-Tazzakki, Bit-Sangi, and *Bit-Kapsi.*   Battanu was king in *Bit-Kapsi*
in 744.   In 737 a new king, Upaš, ruled.   This change of kings may have
had something to do with the new uprising.

the original base of operations, and the various districts mentioned cannot be located with such exactness as to determine the line of march. The country covered was very extensive, and perhaps some of the lands mentioned, especially those already conquered in 744, were brought back into control by the invasion of a few regiments, since garrison posts had been established in 744. It is not to be supposed that the uprising in each district spread over its entire extent.

At any rate, the country from *Bikni*[10] in the far northeast, to *Niqu*[11] in the southwest, was overrun. Perhaps *Niqu* was taken on the return march after crossing over the Pushti-Kuh Mountains. Tiglath Pileser had on his way south thought it necessary to take *Til-Aššur*; and this he reached, if *Ann.* 158 gives the actual route followed, after passing through *Bit-Zualzaš* and *Bit-Matti* (the same order is given in *Pl.* I. 17; *Pl.* II. 19; and *Th. A.* 29). *Til-Aššur* and *Bit-Ištar* reveal by their names that they were originally Assyrian, or were near enough to Assyria to have been incorporated into the Empire, or to have at least retained their Assyrian character. Of course, these names may have been given them after their conquest.[12]

[10] Demavend; according to Sachau, *ZA.* XII. p. 57, it is the Sirdara-Kuh. Demavend is the largest mountain of the range (19,400 ft.). Esarh. IV. 10 describes it as "*Šade uknî,*" which may mean renowned because of its marble and alabaster; but better because of its shining appearance, due to a perpetual covering of ice and snow.

[11] Always "*Niqu (mât) Umliaš.*" Its possession must have been a matter of importance, for it lay immediately west of the outlying hills of the Pushti Kuh and commanded the passes into Elam.

[12] From *Ann.* 176, we learn that it was the seat of a Marduk temple where TP. offered sacrifices. Not only its name makes its location near the Assyrian border probable, but also the fact that TP. sacrificed there. This must have been at the end of the campaign and in celebration of the

Some of the conquered tribes, like the *Bit-Sangibutti*[13] were, as Rost (vol. I. p. XXV) observes, of Babylonian origin ; others were located on the southwestern border of Media.[14] At various places in the district conquered, Tiglath Pileser erected images of his royalty. The spoils of victory included all those productions in which the territory abounded, and as usual Tiglath Pileser did not stint his share. Horses, camels, cattle, mules, "without number I carried away" (*Th. A.* 33). Sixty-five thousand persons were deported to other dependencies.

From the borders of Urarṭu on the north and Rhagian Media[15] on the northeast,[16] to the eastern frontiers of

year's achievements. Of course the end of the campaign found TP. near home. For this reason I cannot agree with Billerbeck, *Sulm.* p. 87, in locating *Til-Aššur* near Kifraur or Gilan. It lay, I think, between *Niqu* and the Diala on the highway into Assyria proper.

[13] *Bit-Sangibutti* near Behistun, *Sulm.* p. 80.

[14] Among these are the peoples whose name is compounded with the element "*Kingi*"; viz., *Kingi-Kangi, Kingi-Alkasiš*. Streck, *ZA.* XV. 338, refuses to see in the element *Kingi* any reminiscence of *Ki-en-gi* = Semitic *Sumer*, but suggests a possible connection with the goddess Kingu of the creation myths. But why Tiele's (*Geschichte*, p. 231) opinion of the preservation in these names of *Ki-en-gi* = lowlands, *i.e.* 'land of reeds,' should be dogmatically rejected I do not see. Rost (vol. I. p. XXVI) refers to Winckler (*Mittl. d. Berl. Ak. Orient. Ver.* 1887, p. 12), who notes that *Kingi* means 'lowlands' as opposed to mountainous districts. This leads him to the observation that these lands on the southwest border of Media were probably largely peopled by a portion of the Sumerians who left their homes and settled here rather than accept the yoke of the Semites when these latter overran Mesopotamia. See IV. R. 9, K. 2861, line 26, where the Assyrian "*ma-at-ti*" is rendered in Sumerian by *Ka-na-ga* (*ka-la-ma*), but where *Ki-en-gi* may also be read.

[15] Delattre, *Le Peuple et l'Empire des Mèdes*, p. 101, correctly equates the region of *Bikni* with Rhagian Media.

[16] On his return march tribute was also received from *I'llipi.* Streck, *ZA.* XV. pp. 380 ff., makes it the country east of the Pushti Kuh ; *i.e.* the northwestern part of the modern Luristan. In *Th. A.* 38, we read (*mât*) *I'l-li-pa-ai u ḫazanatišša šadi-i kali-šu-nu a-di* (*šadu*) *Bi-ik-ni.* This

Babylonia and the boundaries of Assyria proper, Tiglath Pileser was now undisputed master. No enemy was left to contest his supremacy except Sardurri. With him he was now ready to deal. There was in fact no other alternative. Any attempt to penetrate farther west than he had gone in 742–740 and in 738, was not likely to be completely prosperous as long as Sardurri was left unmolested in the rear. In the immediate neighborhood of Urarṭu and in the stretch of country between Lake Van and Lake Urumia on one side, and between Van and Assyria on the south, no vassals were left to Sardurri except perhaps in *Parsua* and *Bustus*, and these were not powerful. The time for Tiglath Pileser to strike at the centre of Urarṭian power had come. He was not the man to delay. In 735 the road led to Ṭurušpa. Sardurri had ventured forth only once, and he had good reason to remember the consequent defeat at *Kištan*. If he would not come forth to battle a second time, Tiglath Pileser must go to him. But it was no easy task; in fact, no Assyrian king ever undertook a more arduous one. To reach Ṭurušpa, the capital of Urarṭu, no approach was feasible, save from the north. On the south the Arjerosh mountains reached almost to the shores of Lake Van. The passes were impossible both because of the snow and the ease with which they could be defended against an invading army, nor was the way *via* the Tigris and the Bitlis-chai and thence west along the shore of the lake easier. The bridle paths along the south shore of the lake were naturally fitted for opposition to a big army. From the south and the east the difficulties were also for-

well describes that part of Luristan and the country all the way to Mt. Demavend, which lies a few miles northeast of modern Teheran.

bidding, for the Khoturdagh Range would have proved
snowy graves for the Assyrian soldiers.   There were but
two possible routes.[17]   One led from the north shore of
Lake Urumia by Tabris and Khoi to Bejazet.   Just
before reaching Bejazet the road turns off southwest to
Lake Van.   The second, the one which Tiglath Pileser
took, led across the Murad-Tschai, between Musch and
Manesgard, then through Dajaini, and northward along
the base of the Sipa Dagh, straight to Lake Van and
Ṭurušpa.   Before reaching Ṭurušpa Tiglath Pileser sent
a detachment to Mt. Birdašu, northwest of Lake Van,
though just what this move was calculated to gain for
him we do not know.   The main body of the troops
ravaged Urarṭu throughout its extent.   Cities and villages
were sacked and the country plundered.   Sardurri was
cooped up in his hill citadel, where he was safe, but as
far as his eye could reach, the track of the Assyrian army
was marked by a line of fire and heaps of ashes.   Ṭurušpa,
however, was impregnable.   Tiglath Pileser could not
starve out the garrison without a fleet to cut off the food
supply that came into the citadel by way of the lake.

At the base of the citadel hill Tiglath Pileser set up
the image of his royalty and turned back homeward.   Sardurri lived, but Urarṭu's power was dead.   Ruaš, son of
Sardurri, rebuilt Ṭurušpa on an even more impregnable
rock, and we find him in conflict with Sargon some years
later, but as far as danger to Assyrian supremacy was
concerned, Urarṭu could henceforth be safely disregarded.
Assyria had vindicated her right to the mastery of Western
Asia.

To the west or the south, as occasion might demand

[17] Cf. Belck, ZA. IX. p. 350.

Tiglath Pileser could now turn his attention without fear of the foe who had up to 735 obstructed every step. We have seen how in the following years, 734–732, this freedom from Sardurri's influence made the western campaign easy. Now but one foe of account remained. From the Mediterranean to *Mt. Bikni* and the Caspian on the north, and from Judah to farthest Media on the south, Assyria was supreme. It only remained for Tiglath Pileser to gain the crown of Babylon, and Assyria would be without a rival state in Asia Minor.

CHAPTER VI[1]

THE CONQUEST OF BABYLONIA

For Tiglath Pileser III to gain the crown of Babylonia
was to acquire the unique distinction of being the first
Assyrian king to rule simultaneously in both countries.
There can be no doubt that this had been his aim from
the very beginning, and its achievement marks him as the
greatest of Assyrian conquerors. Nor had his ambition
outrun his power to accomplish a wonderful work. Of
all the nations in Western Asia only Babylonia retained a
measure of real autonomy, and of that autonomy the
Babylonians were exceedingly proud and jealous. Tiglath
Pileser, because his vast empire was at peace, might be
prepared to "grasp the hands of Bel." But it is doubt-
ful whether or not the Babylonians would have been
equally anxious to welcome him as their king, had all
been well with them. Perhaps internal trouble would not
have been sufficient excuse for Tiglath Pileser to march
south into Babylon in 729, as he had done in the first
year of his reign. At any rate, he waited until a disrup-
tion of government in Babylonia led to the interference of
the Chaldeans in Babylonian affairs ; and fortune played
into his hands. In 730 Tiglath Pileser was prepared for
any eventuality, for there was no disturbance in any part

[1] The sources are *Pl.* I. 13–14 ; *Th. A.* 15–28 ; *Babyln. King List,*
col. IV. lines 5–8 ; *Babyln. Chron.* col. I. 17–23 ; cf. above, Chapter I.
p. 6; *Babyln. Chron.* B. Col. I. 1–26, and cf. *KB.*[2] p. 275.

of his wide realm.   Babylon alone was in a ferment. From 745 and up to his death, Nabunâçir had remained loyal to Tiglath Pileser.   But in all probability there always existed a pro-Babylonian party in Babylon, which had never ceased to agitate against the overlordship of Assyria, and had rendered Nabunâçir's reign precarious. The fact that *Borsippa* revolted is significant, for it was one of the cities captured by Tiglath Pileser in 745.

Nabunâçir was succeeded by Nabû-nâdin-zir, who, after a very brief reign, was killed by Nabû-šum-ukîn, an usurper.   He was perhaps successful in his usurpation because the anti-Assyrian party were his sponsors.   Throughout all this turmoil of rapid regnal and dynastic change Tiglath Pileser remained at home, watchful and apparently passive.   As long as the strife in Babylonia was purely domestic he had no urgent need to fear for his own plans ; but soon the inevitable happened.   The Chaldeans, who never allowed an opportunity of gaining a foothold in Babylonia to escape them, took advantage of the disturbed conditions of government.   Their most powerful tribe, the *Bit-Ammukani,* under the leadership of Ukinzîr,[2] entered Babylon.   Ukînzir proclaimed himself king.   Tiglath Pileser's excuse had come.   As the suzerain of Babylon, he was her natural protector from foreign foes, and he could not allow the always dangerous Chaldeans to come into such threatening proximity to the Assyrian border line.   If no Babylonian could hold the throne, certainly neither must a Chaldean be permitted to do so.

Tiglath Pileser marches south, his objective point being *Šapia,* the capital of Ukînzir and the metropolis of the

[2] Cf. Chapter I. p. 6.   Cf. Esarh. Cyln. II. 42–43 (*KB*.[2] p. 128).

Bit-Ammukani. *En route* he conquered the *Puqudu* [3] and thoroughly subjugated them. Their cities, *Ḫilimmu* and *Pillutu,* were sacked [4] and the whole district placed under a governor whose seat of administration was at *Arrapha.* [5] A large number of the inhabitants of the conquered territory were transported into Assyria and settled there in scattered colonies. The *Silani* people fared even worse. *Nabû-ušabši,* their king, was killed, and *Sarrabani,* his royal city, ruined, while the cities of *Tarbaçu* and *Iabullu* were added to the number of ash heaps left in the wake of the destroyer. The whole territory gave up 55,000 prisoners.

Next came the *Bit-Sa'alli.* Their king must in some way have perjured himself (*Th. A.* 19). He retreated into his capital, *Dûr-Illatai,* which he fortified, but to no

---

[3] The *Puqudu* are not mentioned in *Pl.* II. 6, or in *Th. A.* 13. It is possible to include them in the list of peoples conquered in 745, but in view of their having been the most important Aramean tribe, it is strange that they should not be mentioned in the *Annals. Th. A.* arranged, of course, geographically, enumerates the conquests of 745 and 731 together. I think it best fits the known facts to assign the expedition against the *Puqudu* to the latter year. The *Puqudu* were located on the extreme eastern borders of Elam. They are the Pekod of Jer. l. 21. It has been claimed that the name Pekod in that passage is only symbolical and not a proper noun, since the term mentioned with it, Merathaim, is certainly figurative, meaning "double rebellion." But Ez. xxiii. 23 disproves this claim. There Pekod, Šutu, and Kutu are mentioned in connection with the Assyrians. Talmud, Ḥulin, 107 a, mentions a *Nahr Peko* in the vicinity of a city called *Nerš.*

[4] Whether *I-di-bi-ri-i-na* is a proper name is in doubt. Rost (vol. I. p. 57) is undecided. He transliterates the text (*Th. A.* 13), *ša I-di-bi-ri-i-na,* and in the translation simply repeats the same words ; nor does he give the word a place in his index of proper names. Schrader, *KB.*[2] 33, reads " *ša idi bi-ri-i-na (maḫaza) Ḫi-li-im-mu* "; and translates, "which on the side of the *biriina* of the city *Ḫilimmu.*" Strong, *RP.* V. p. 121, reads, "*ša idi biri ina Khilummu,*" translating, "which (looks) towards the midst of the city of *Khilummu.*"

[5] Near Tuz-Khurmah ; cf. Scheil in *Rec. d. Trav.* p. 186.

purpose. The city was obliged to surrender, and together with *Amlilatu*, rendered up its treasure and contributed its large quota to the 50,400 prisoners who were parcelled out into widely distributed settlements. But the city which Tiglath Pileser was most anxious to take, *Šapia*, successfully resisted every siege device. All its surrounding country was devastated, but Ukînzir retained his capital, at least for the time being. To complete the subjugation of the Chaldeans was impossible while Ukînzir remained unsubdued, but all the rest of the tribes were made tributary. Balasu, too, of the *Dakkuri*,[6] sent tokens of submission; while Merodach Baladan [7] of the *Bit-Yakin*, a country no king of which had ever done homage to Assyria (*Th. A.* 26), journeyed to Tiglath Pileser's camp while the latter was besieging *Šapia*, and rendered his voluntary tribute of precious metals and the products of his swampland country. To the list of subject princes was added Nadin of *Larrak*.[8] All that now stood between Tiglath Pileser and the throne of Babylon, was Ukînzir. To achieve his ambition, the *Bit-Amukkani* and their leader had to be put out of the way. The year 730 Tiglath Pileser spent at home, preparing for the final campaign.

[6] Usually *Bît-Dakkuri* (Esarh. II. 42) (*mâtu*) *Bît-Dak-kur-i ša ki-rib* (*mâtu*) *Kal-di ai-ab Ba-bi-lu ka-mu-u.* "*Bît-Dakkuri* in Chaldea, inimical to Babylon." West of the Euphrates near Babylon and Borsippa. It is mentioned together with all the tribes which TP. mentions in 731, in Sargon, *Prunk.* 21 (*KB.*[2] p. 55): *Ša mi-ṣir* (*mâtu*) *Elamtu* (*mâtu*) *Karduniaš i-liš u šap-liš* (*mâtu*) *Bît-Amukkani* (*mâtu*) *Bît-Dak-ku-ri* (*mâtu*) *Bît-Si-la-ni* (*mâtu*) *Bît-Sa'al-la si-ḫir-ti* (*mâtu*) *Kal-di ma-la-ba-šu-u*, "In the district of Elam throughout its whole extent . . . all of Elam as much as it is."

[7] The form Berodach Baladan in 2 K. xx. 12 is a textual corruption.

[8] Lenormant, *La Langue Primitive*, p. 34, identifies it with the Ellasar of Gen. xiv. 1. According to Loftus, "Travels and Researches," p. 256, it is identical with the ruins of Sankereh.

In all likelihood, this interval of preparation was a busy time in diplomacy and intrigue. Even with Ukinzir out of the way, there was still an anti-Assyrian party in Baby-lon, who could be depended upon to resist to the last the crowning of a foreigner. These pro-Babylonians would accept Tiglath Pileser's aid in freeing their country of the Chaldean danger, but would insist on having a native sov-ereign. How did the always powerful priesthood stand in the matter? In 745, while a native king ruled, they had hailed Tiglath Pileser as king of Assyria, and as such had brought him gifts for clearing their country of her enemies. Would they accept him as king of their own land in 729? To ascertain their attitude with surety Tiglath Pileser during his stay at home in 730, probably carried on nego-tiations with the priests. Perhaps the defeat of Ukinzir was part of the price which the priests exacted in exchange for any aid they might promise to render to the Assyrian king, in his efforts to gain the Babylonian crown. Cyrus in later times probably gained just such an easy access to Babylon because of a previous compact with the priest-hood, and it demands no great stretch of the imagination to think that Tiglath Pileser too had a perfectly clear un-derstanding with the priestly caste. At any rate in 729 he proceeded south a second time, and this time his operations against *Šapia* were successful. Ukinzir was captured and of course executed. The way to the throne of Babylon was now clear. On the New Year's day Tiglath Pileser III " grasped the hands of Bel," and was crowned under the name of Pulu. *De facto* and *de jure* king of Assyria, king of Sumer and Akkad, conqueror of Western Asia, a prince without rival, the usurper of 745 has become the master of civilization.

Great pity it is that the records are mutilated. Were the sources not so meagre, a fuller knowledge would perhaps compel us to class Tiglath Pileser III as the equal of Cyrus, than whom the Eastern world produced no mightier warrior and administrator. From the Caspian to Egypt, all of Asia was dependent upon Assyria. No future king would hold his empire more firmly than Tiglath Pileser had held it, nor inspire greater respect and fear of his mighty power. In 728 Tiglath Pileser repeated the ceremony of coronation at Babylon, and in 727, in the month of Tebet, he died. His son, Shalmaneser IV, succeeded him, but the dynasty was short-lived, for Shalmaneser ruled but five years, and in 722 the stranger Sargon founded a new line. He, too, was a usurper, his succession to the throne resulting from a reaction to the tendencies which had been responsible for the elevation of Tiglath Pileser. The latter king's reign was only of comparatively brief duration, but it sufficed him to make Assyria strong enough to endure until her cultural work for civilization was finished. In modern eyes that must constitute his chief glory.

During his reign he had time to build but one palace, and that, as has been noted, was dismantled by Esarhaddon. But better than a palace, he builded an empire, far-flung, but well governed and fairly compact, despite the heterogeneous elements of which it was composed. The central problem of Assyrian statecraft was to weld the subject races and peoples into a homogeneous unit. Such a task was never fully accomplished, either by Assyria or by any of the great world powers that succeeded her, but Tiglath Pileser approximated to it sufficiently well to erect a structure far more stable than that of any of his predecessors and to render Assyria safe until her work was done.

After he had conquered a territory, he, like his predecessors, placed it under the administrative supervision of the governor of the immediately adjoining province, or else made an entirely new province out of it. Tiglath Pileser's innovation consisted in this: whereas former kings had colonized a newly acquired land with settlers from Assyria proper, and had placed portions of the conquered subjects in scattered colonies throughout Assyria, he kept his Assyrian subjects at home. His empire was too extensive to do otherwise. Had he colonized subject lands with Assyrians he must soon have depleted the native and homogeneous population of the home country. Instead, he effected a transfer of subjugated peoples from one dependency to a far distant one. His aim was to keep Assyria intact and thus to minimize the danger of rebellion and revolt. He allowed no colony of foreign settlers to be large enough or near enough to one of their own affiliation to permit the possibility of any concerted action against the imperial government. The colonies were so located that their thought-habit, their customs, their religion, and even their language made them, if not offensive to their new neighbors, at least a segregated unit among them. No collusion, in fact, no bond of sympathy between the old and the new population was possible. It might even happen that an uprising on the part of the old settlers would operate to attach the new colonists more closely to Assyria. For the first step in a rebellion is generally a demonstration against the stranger within the gates. In the event of such demonstrations the new settler would have no recourse but to appeal to Assyria. He had no

greater love for Assyria than had the strangers among
whom he had been settled, but to feed fat his grudge and
nurse vengeance would in no wise answer his need of self-
preservation. Assyria had to be petitioned for help, and
granting it, came naturally to be regarded as a deliverer.
Thus a measure of real loyalty was secured, and it was
probably in this way that Panammu of *Sam'al* was rendered
faithful. The Assyrian army was never so numerous as
to permit large detachments to be stationed at garrison
posts. At most, a governor might have a small company
to aid him in the enforcement of his authority. The
realization that Assyria was ready to back up her officials
might not deter a determined people from revolt. If the
rebellion arose in a district far from Assyria, aid might be
long in coming and the uprising have assumed very serious
proportions before its arrival; but with Tiglath Pileser's
plan in effect there was a colony of strange settlers on the
spot. These had no affiliations with the indigenous population and could readily be pressed into service to aid
the governor until reënforcements arrived. It is more
than probable that this plan of colonization resulted in
furnishing a source of recruiting for the army which obviated too great a drain upon the male portion of Assyrian
population. With only a fair-sized force from home, a
considerable contingent of vassals could be enlisted *en
route* to the seat of disturbance, together with a number
of troops from among the foreign colonists in the vicinity.

It was this system of colonization that gave Assyria the
lease of life which she enjoyed. It might even have in-
sured her a longer national existence, had she not been
far too small to hold out against the barbarians who later
on overran Babylonia and put an end to its career. To

his high ability as a warrior, and the glory with which he
graced his country's name, there must be ascribed to
Tiglath Pileser III as his greatest credit, that administrative system which conserved the existence of the Empire
until Babylon once again came into her own.

COLUMBIA UNIVERSITY PRESS

Columbia University in the City of New York

COLUMBIA UNIVERSITY CONTRIBUTIONS TO ORIENTAL HISTORY AND PHILOLOGY

Edited by RICHARD J. H. GOTTHEIL and JOHN DYNELEY PRINCE

No. I. SUMERIAN HYMNS

From Cuneiform Texts in the British Museum. Transliteration, translation, and commentary. By FREDERICK VANDERBURGH, Ph.D. 8vo, pp. xii + 83. Price, paper, $1.00; cloth, $1.50 *net*.

No. II. THE HISTORY OF THE GOVERNORS OF EGYPT

By ABU UMAR MUHAMMAD IBN YUSUF AL-KINDI. Edited from a unique manuscript in the British Museum. By NICHOLAS AUGUST KOENIG, Ph.D. 8vo, paper, pp. 33 + 33. Price, $1.00 *net*.

No. III. ASSYRIAN PRIMER

An Inductive Method of Learning the Cuneiform Signs. By J. DYNELEY PRINCE, Ph.D., Professor of Semitic Languages, Columbia University. 8vo, paper, pp. 58. Price, $1.00 *net*.

No. IV. THE WITNESS OF THE VULGATE, PESHITTA AND SEPTUAGINT TO THE TEXT OF ZEPHANIAH

By SIDNEY ZANDSTRA, Ph.D. 8vo, paper, pp. 52. Price, $1.00 *net*.

No. V. TIGLATH PILESER III

By ABRAHAM S. ANSPACHER, Ph.D. 8vo, cloth, pp. xvi + 72. Price, $1.25 *net*.

LEMCKE & BUECHNER, AGENTS

30-32 WEST 27th ST., NEW YORK